HIKES ▶ Around Philadelphia

HIKES
Around
Philadelphia

Boyd Newman & Linda Newman

Temple University Press
Philadelphia, Pennsylvania

Temple University Press, Philadelphia 19122
Copyright ©1997 by Temple University
All rights reserved
Published 1997
Printed in the United States of America

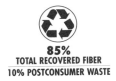

85%
TOTAL RECOVERED FIBER
10% POSTCONSUMER WASTE

This book is printed on acid-free paper
for greater longevity

Text Design: Ox + Company, Inc.

Library of Congress Cataloging–in–Publication Data

Newman, Boyd, 1941–   .
  Hikes Around Philadelphia/Boyd Newman and Linda Newman.
  p. cm.
  1. Hiking—Pennsylvania—Philadelphia Region—Guidebooks.
  2. Trails—Pennsylvania—Philadelphia Region—Guidebooks.
  3. Natural history—Pennsylvania—Philadelphia Region—
    Guidebooks.
  4. Philadelphia Region (Pa.)—Guidebooks.
    I. Newman, Linda A., 1943–   . II. Title.
  GV199.42.P4P556 1997
  796.51'09748'11—dc21   96-51501
                                              CIP

ISBN 1-56639-529-1 (cloth); 1-56639-530-5 (paper)

Contents

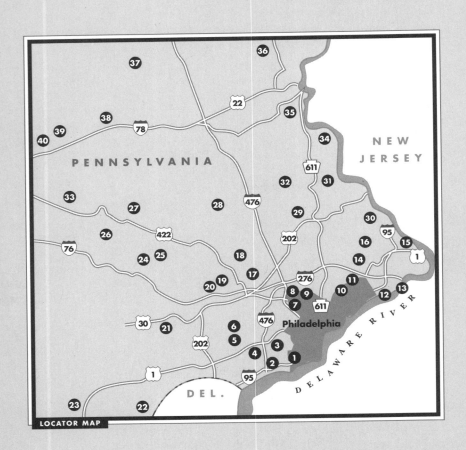

Appendices

Introduction

When people think of Philadelphia, they think of commerce, education, culture, and industry. They probably do not associate Philadelphia and the Delaware Valley with nature and the out-of-doors. Perhaps they should.

There is an abundance of natural places to explore in and around Philadelphia. Within only an hour or so of the city limits, you can find dense forests on isolated mountain ridges; bogs and swamps; wide-open meadows; rivers, streams, waterfalls, and lakes. Scattered here and there is evidence of early farmsteads and pre-industrial settlements. You can clamber across a ringing boulder field from the last ice age. Or you can visit the restored homes and trails hiked by John James Audubon and Daniel Boone. By walking quietly through the habitats of a wide variety of birds and animals, you may also be fortunate enough to observe at close hand the wildlife that thrives in the Philadelphia area.

This book is intended to introduce you to some of these delights. The trails described range from 1.0 to 12.6 miles in length. They are suitable for the novice hiker in average physical condition, although for such a person we recommend a few of the shorter hikes to start. At the beginning of each description we have included introductory information to help you decide where to hike first, or where to go after a week of rain, or where to take your visiting in-laws. Once you get started, you may find you want to do them all.

Distance The total distance in miles is given for each hike. Sometimes it is possible to shorten or lengthen a hike; if so, these directions are included, although we have not indicated such changes in the mileage totals. In deciding how difficult the hike is likely to be, you should couple mileage information with the information about elevation. Five miles on the flat may seem much easier than a 3-mile hike, half of which is uphill.

Elevation Elevation refers to cumulative gains in elevation—in other words, how much climbing is included in the hike. The total may accrue from one long uphill climb or several shorter ones.

Time to hike We offer only an estimate of the time required for a person in average condition to walk the distance. Most people can walk a mile in 20 to 30 minutes, depending on how rocky the trail is. Add another 30 minutes for each gain of 1000 feet in elevation. These estimates do not include rest stops or breaks for birdwatching or exploring along the trail. We suggest that when people hike together, they have the slower person lead on the trail. It is not enjoyable to be continually struggling to keep up. Also, be sure to allow enough time to return to your car before dark.

Surface There are some very rocky trails in Pennsylvania, especially along the Appalachian Trail. Sometimes you may need to cross a stream on stepping stones. For hikes like these, boots with ankle support are essential. For other surfaces you can probably get by with comfortable walking shoes or sneakers.

Interesting features Each hike has been chosen because of some unusual or interesting feature. Some hikes may have historic interest. Others feature unusual terrain, geologic formations, interesting flora and fauna, or other special characteristics.

Facilities We have included information on the availability of water, rest rooms, and picnic facilities. Do not drink from a stream or lake; you have no way of knowing the water purity.

Disability access We did not select these hikes for disability access, but information on access is included for those who may be interested. Of the forty hikes, thirteen have some accessibility and five are completely accessible from start to finish. (See Appendix B, Hikes by Disability Access.)

Hunting Pennsylvania is a major hunting state, especially for deer. It is unsafe to be out in the woods when hunters are around, especially in state game lands during deer season.

Fall is a beautiful time of year to hike, but it is also the most common time for hunting. The Pennsylvania Game Commission sets game hunting seasons each year. In general, the season for big game (bear, deer, turkey) runs from the last week of November to the first week of January. Bow hunting begins the last week of September and lasts till the first week of January. Small game season (squirrel, grouse, rabbit, pheasant, quail, raccoon, fox) runs from mid-October to the last week of January. There is also spring hunting for turkey in May.

Happily for hikers, hunting is not allowed anywhere in Pennsylvania on Sundays. Except on Sundays, during hunting season you should not hike on state game lands or in other areas where hunting is allowed. Wear blaze orange at all times of the year when hiking on game lands.

Fortunately, hunting is not permitted at all on many of the trails described here.

Directions to trailhead   In using the directions for driving to the start of each hike, first refer to the locator map, which will help you find each hike in relationship to your own location. Detailed directions to each trailhead begin from a major road and nearby community. Except where noted, the directions work traveling from either direction on the major road.

Safety on the trail   The difficulty of each hike depends on distance, elevation changes, and trail surface. You will find, as we did, that as you become better conditioned, you will be able to hike greater distances. Do not attempt one of the longer and more arduous hikes at first. These hikes are intended for your enjoyment. Begin with a short hike on a level surface. From this beginning you should be able to tell whether you can progress rapidly to more difficult hikes or move gradually through the intermediate hikes first. (See Appendix A, Hikes by Length.)

These hikes are located in national forests, state game lands, state parks, county parks, and wildlife refuges. In general, the trails are well blazed and maintained. However, do remain alert for trail markings. Double blazes indicate a turn. Equestrian trails are often marked with strips of yellow or orange plastic at the rider's eye level, about ten feet off the ground. Be prepared for changes from the routes described here; sometimes trails are relocated. Do not walk past "no trespassing" or "private property" signs.

In the unlikely event you find yourself off the trail, backtrack until you find the blazes again. If that fails, follow a stream or power line cut; these will lead you eventually to a road.

Hiking is a generally safe activity, but there are certain hazards in the out-of-doors that are not encountered elsewhere. These warnings should not discourage you from hiking, but you need to remain aware of the risks to avoid unpleasant or even dangerous situations.

Insects In moist areas when temperatures are warm, Pennsylvania mosquitoes can be ferocious. Come prepared. Insect repellent containing deet can be applied directly to skin. Repellents containing permethrin should not be used on the skin but are effective on clothing; be sure to reapply frequently.

Gnats, or "no-see'ums," are frequently a nuisance in late summer. They are attracted to moisture in your exhaled breath and to your eyes. A visor or hat with a bill to which you apply insect repellent containing permethrin does seem to keep them away from your face.

People who are allergic to bees and wasps should always carry the appropriate emergency kit when hiking.

A most serious insect threat is a bite from a deer tick infected with the bacteria that causes Lyme disease. The deer tick is very small, and its bite may go undetected. An early symptom of Lyme disease is an unusual splotchy rash, which is easily treated with antibiotics. Later, more serious symptoms can include cardiac and neurologic problems, as well as arthritis. Lyme disease at all stages requires treatment by a physician.

Recently, two new tick-borne illnesses, human granulocytic ehrlichiosis (HGE) and babesiosis, have been reported in several states, including Pennsylvania. These are quite serious diseases with severe flu-like symptoms and a fairly high reported death rate. Unlike Lyme disease, which can be treated with several antibiotics, HGE is sensitive only to tetracycline; babesiosis may respond to quinine plus an antibiotic. These diseases also require medical attention.

The first line of defense against all tick-borne diseases is to wear a long-sleeved shirt and long pants and to use effective insect repellents. The second line of defense is to inspect your own skin and, if possible, have someone help you in checking your neck, the backs of your legs, and your back when you return to your car. An infected tick must be attached to you for many hours to pass infection on. If you find a tick, remove it immediately, including mouthparts, with tweezers. If symptoms occur—whether you detect a tick or not—see your doctor.

Animal hazards Snakes will not seek a confrontation with you, but they do not like to be disturbed, either. You are most likely to encounter them sunning on warm rocks. When hiking or climbing on rocky terrain, be careful where you put your hands and feet. Wear hiking boots, which offer some protection, when you are hiking in such areas.

Rabies is endemic in many wild animals, especially squirrels, foxes, raccoons, and bats. Avoid any animal, wild or domestic, that acts strangely or seems unafraid of you.

Hypo- or hyperthermia Becoming either overheated or chilled can be risky for the hiker. To prevent either situation, dress appropriately for the weather. Consider dressing in layers so that you can adjust your clothing to changes in temperature or weather. In cold weather, take along an extra pair of socks in case your feet get wet. Carry a small bottle of water with you on longer hikes, and remember to drink plenty of liquids, especially in warm weather. If rain is a possibility, take a poncho and waterproof hat to keep you dry.

Lightning During thunderstorms, do not seek shelter under a tall tree, especially at the top of a ridgeline. Whenever possible, move to a lower elevation and seek shelter under a group of smaller trees.

Poison ivy Some people develop severe allergic reactions to any exposure at all to poison ivy, oak, or sumac; others seem immune or experience only a mild, localized rash. The best way to avoid the discomfort is to learn to recognize the plants and avoid them.

Poison ivy and oak varieties exhibit compound leaves divided in three leaflets and grow as a climbing or trailing vine, a shrub, or a ground plant, several inches to 2 feet high. Poison sumac has seven to thirteen alternate leaflets and grows as a small tree 6 to 20 feet high; in the spring the leaves are shiny and light green, becoming dark green in the summer. In the fall, all three plants produce white berries, and the leaves turn colorful shades of red. They seem to prefer damp soil and the light-to-medium shade along trails.

Long pants and long-sleeved shirts offer good protection. However, the sap, or urushiol, can remain on clothing or pet fur and later can then be transferred to your skin, producing the reaction. Removing the urushiol immediately with plain water, before the reaction has set in, can prevent the rash. Severe cases may require an oral dose or an injection of cortisone, either available by doctor's prescription.

General safety   Whenever you set out on a hike, let someone know where you are going. Hike alone only for short distances in well-traveled areas; for all other hiking excursions, we recommend you hike with a companion.

Footwear and clothing   When choosing footwear for any hike, consider both the terrain you will encounter and any personal history of injury and weakness in your feet, ankles, knees, hips, or back. When the sole of your foot strikes the ground, the impact is transmitted through your weight-bearing joints. These joints not only absorb the forces, they must also adjust your posture, maintaining your center of balance over your base of support. The joints of the ankle and feet are normally quite well suited to accommodate the demands of uneven terrain. They allow the postural adjustments necessary to maintain your dynamic balance.

Pennsylvania's rockier and steeper trails place additional stress on ankle joints to repeatedly absorb these forces. For most people, stabilizing the ankle with a high-top boot helps to prevent injury and improve comfort. However, a stabilized (immobile) ankle transmits forces to the knee, hip, and back, forcing these less flexible joints to adapt. If you have a history of knee injury, consider wearing a brace to support the knee and a low-top or soft high-top boot to allow more ankle flexibility.

Fit is most important. When you shop for hiking shoes or boots, try to find an experienced salesperson. After you have made your purchase, wear your hiking footwear around the house for a few days to test them and break them in. Most stores will allow you to return boots that have not been worn outside. Do not set out on a hike wearing brand-new shoes or boots.

The clothing you should wear on a hike depends on the weather and the season. In cold temperatures, dress in layers. Dressing to protect yourself against hypo- or hyperthermia is discussed above. In all seasons and weather conditions, we also recommend that you wear a long-sleeved shirt and long pants, for four very good reasons—protection from scratches, ticks, mosquitoes, and poison ivy.

What to take along For the hikes in this book under 10 miles, you do not need to carry a backpack; a waist or fanny pack should be enough, unless you plan to carry a meal with you.

Water is an absolute essential, whatever the

weather or distance. Light snack food or a sandwich is welcome for hikes over about 5 miles. A compass and watch come in handy. For the allergic, a bee sting kit is also essential.

The need for other equipment depends on the weather and the season. From spring to first frost, take along insect repellent. Even in the winter and spring, when there may be little shade even in the woods, sun screen is useful. A hat or visor provides sun protection and shades the eyes. Optional items include small cameras, binoculars, and field guides for identifying birds, plants, or trees.

The latest in navigation aids for the high-tech hiker is a global positioning system, or GPS. A hand-held receiver collects signals from a constellation of navigation satellites. The device then computes a position fix, in latitude, longitude, and altitude, for anywhere on earth. Additional features of the GPS allow you to compute and continuously update your position, and set and navigate a route. These devices are now priced at less than $200, and with competition the price is likely to fall even further. For your convenience, we have included the coordinates for each trailhead, which you may find useful in locating the start of each hike. For Hike 26, Nolde Forest, we have added intermediate coordinates that you can use to navigate along the entire hike route.

Finally, don't forget a trail map! The ones we have provided will be fine. In the descriptions of individual hikes, we have also described any maps or guides that are available at the site. State Game Lands maps are available by writing to the State Game Commission, Dept. MS, 2001 Elmerton Avenue, Harrisburg, PA 17120-9797, or Southeast Region Headquarters, Box 2584, R.D. #2, Reading, PA 19605. The maps are $1.00 each including tax; specify which game land map you are requesting.

We think you will find that the experience of

hiking is both challenging and enjoyable. Hiking provides physical exercise, the direct experience of nature, and the fun of discovering what lies just around the bend. You may find that you decide to go on a hike for one reason and then continue hiking for many others. Let this book be your guide. Many interesting places ready for your discovery are close by.

Note to the hiker Trails and trail conditions often change. Although the information here is accurate to the best of our knowledge, hikers should be aware that conditions may be different at the time of their hike and prepare for that possibility.

HIKES ▶ Around Philadelphia

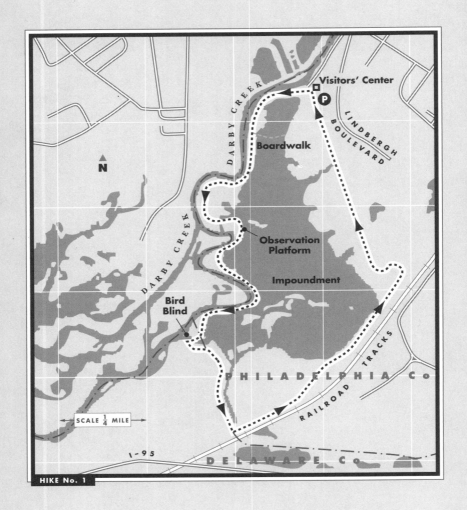

N

Visitors' Center

LINDBERGH BOULEVARD

Boardwalk

DARBY CREEK

DARBY CREEK

Observation
Platform

Impoundment

Bird
Blind

PHILADELPHIA Co

RAILROAD TRACKS

SCALE ⅟₄ MILE

I - 95

DELAWARE Co

HIKE No. 1

Heinz Wildlife Refuge

John Heinz National Wildlife Refuge at Tinicum
86th Street and Lindbergh Boulevard
Philadelphia, PA 19113
(215) 365-3118

Distance	3.2 miles
Elevation	less than 10 feet
Time to hike	1½ hours
Surface	dirt, gravel and grass, wide two-track; can be muddy in early spring
Interesting features	only National Wildlife Refuge in eastern Pennsylvania; 1,200 acres of fresh-water tidal and nontidal marsh, fields, and woodlands, all within the city limits of Philadelphia; on the migratory route for waterfowl and thus a nesting and feeding site; nature walks and programs
Facilities	water, rest rooms in visitors' center, many benches along trail; no picnic facilities; wear long pants and long-sleeved shirt to protect against poison ivy, mosquitoes, and ticks, and wear insect repellent
Disability access	The wide, level trail is wheelchair accessible; permission for persons with disabilities to drive through the preserve on the Impoundment Trail obtainable at the visitors' center
Hunting	no

Directions **from I-95 traveling north:**

1. take exit 10 (PA 291–airport), drive east for 1.0 mile to Bartram Avenue, turn left
2. drive 1.6 miles to 84th Street, turn left
3. drive 0.7 mile on 84th to Lindbergh Boulevard, turn left
4. drive 0.2 mile on Lindbergh to the refuge on the right

from I-95 traveling south:

1. take exit 12 (Bartram Avenue), drive north for 1.4 miles to 84th Street, turn right
2. drive 0.7 mile on 84th to Lindbergh Boulevard, turn left
3. drive 0.2 mile on Lindbergh to the refuge on the right

Coordinates 39°53'32"N; 75°15'26"W

The Heinz National Wildlife Refuge is a tidal fresh-water marsh, a wide, flat wetland close enough to the ocean to be under tidal influences, yet the water is fresh, not salt. It is the habitat of many types of birds, especially waterfowl and wading birds, and it is the largest remaining example of this type of ecosystem in eastern Pennsylvania. It has been underappreciated for many years, considered fit only as a landfill site, but has been largely rehabilitated through efforts of the U.S. Fish and Wildlife Service, and many volunteers.

The visitors' center, a small stone building, is staffed by a guide from the Fish and Wildlife Service who offers maps, information on recent bird sightings, and friendly advice on the trail conditions. The trail begins to the left of the visitors' center. This pleasant, easy hike is well marked. Keep the impoundment to your left and you will have no chance of getting lost. The trail as described is 3.2 miles long. If you would like a longer hike of 8.5

miles, ask for the map of the entire refuge. The longer hike will take you directly through the marsh on a ten-foot-wide berm adjacent to Darby Creek. You also have the option of taking a shorter loop by using the boardwalk described below.

The Impoundment Trail is easy, level walking on a dike; the fresh water impoundment is to your left and Darby Creek is on your right. Darby Creek is under tidal influences; there is a difference of about 5 feet between high and low tide at the visitors' center. Behind the center is the launch point for a 4.5-mile canoe trail, navigable only at high tide. High tide actually reverses the flow of the creek, into the marsh. At low tide the water flows back into Darby Creek from the marsh.

After walking past some benches, note a gate to your left and one straight ahead. The gate to the left marks your return route. Continue straight ahead on the Impoundment Trail. At 0.25 mile you pass a boardwalk across the northern end of the impoundment. You may take this across for a short loop walk of 0.75 mile. This short route is easy walking but not really disability accessible because of the nine steps down to reach the boardwalk from the Impoundment Trail.

Continuing on the main trail, you will encounter a large two-tier observation platform at 0.75 mile. A changing display features posters on the wildlife to be found at each time of year. Nesting boxes along both sides of the trail (at the impoundment and along Darby Creek) attract a variety of birds.

In winter you may see white-tailed deer, Canada geese, northern harriers (marsh hawks), song sparrows and chickadees, northern mockingbirds, sea gulls, and small mammals including rabbits, raccoons, squirrels, and foxes. In spring and summer you may see waterfowl that nest here: grebes, teals, wood ducks, common pintails, and northern shovelers, as well as wading birds, including species of heron, egret, and ibis. Migrating warblers pass through in large numbers in the spring and fall.

As you continue on the trail you will see that Darby Creek on the right widens to a tidal marsh at 1.0 mile. Mulberry trees, honeysuckle shrubs, and blackberries line the trail and attract many songbirds. At 1.2 miles you reach a bird blind, a good spot to view the birds there. Tree swallows compete for the nesting boxes. Red-winged blackbirds and American goldfinches are also common.

The well-marked trail turns sharply left. (You would continue straight ahead to follow the longer walk through the marsh.) The marsh on your right was used as a landfill from 1956 to 1974; this interesting wetland habitat was considered as nothing more than a dump and a mosquito-breeding nuisance. An underground pipeline also passes through the refuge. These disturbances to the natural environment have resulted in the proliferation of giant reed or phragmite, a 6- to 8-foot tall grassy weed with brown plumes, which has taken over much of the marsh. Efforts have been made to dredge a channel through some of the area and create ponds. The purpose is to encourage native plant species, such as cattails, sedges, and rushes, which provide a better variety of food and cover for wildlife.

On the impoundment side, the problem is an overabundance of spatterdock. Spatterdock, which grows in the water and has large, glossy leaves and a yellow flower, by June may cover up to 30 percent of the impoundment. An experiment of the Fish and Wildlife Service in 1994 to control it by a "dewatering" project using a water bladder was not effective because Darby Creek flooded the drained area of the impoundment. In the latest control effort, two test plots were sprayed with "Rodeo," or glyphosate, an enzyme inhibiter, followed by the aerial spraying of 80 acres. This allows the preferred wildlife vegetation to germinate. Spraying seems to be a control method that will work.

Purple loosestrife, a plant introduced by European settlers in the early 1800s, has also spread, crowding out other plants and reducing diversity. It is a poor source of food and cover for wetland wildlife. Five species of weevil and beetles that feed on the plant have been propagated at Tinicum, and it is hoped that these insects will limit the spread of this plant.

Botulism, a fatal bacterial food poisoning, is sometimes a serious problem at Tinicum. Shore birds, at the top of the food chain, are especially susceptible to the toxin produced by this bacteria, which proliferates in stagnant ponds where species on which the birds feed thrive. If botulism recurs, the water level of the impoundment can be somewhat controlled by pumping water from the impoundment to the creek, or allowing the flow of water from the creek into the impoundment.

The trail again turns sharply to the left. This next section could be nicknamed "planes, trains, and automobiles." Railroad tracks lie only 70 feet away to the right; just beyond is traffic on I-95; and beyond that, you can see airplanes flying into and out of Philadelphia International Airport. After only a few hundred feet, though, these signs of civilization fade away. You can see many inlets to the left, and several trails will take you directly to the water's edge. The edge of the impoundment looks rather swamplike, with water-loving trees such as willows, alders, locusts, and red ("swamp") maples. Insects abound, as well as the birds that feed on them. There are also at least fifty species of wildflowers that bloom here at various times. In spring and summer, especially, you can see many varieties of butterflies as well. The mourning cloak butterfly, dark purple-brown with wings edged in yellow and with bright blue spots, is the earliest to appear in March.

At 3.0 miles, you will pass a trail to the left that leads to the eastern end of the boardwalk over the impoundment. At 3.2 miles, you return to the visitors' center and the parking area.

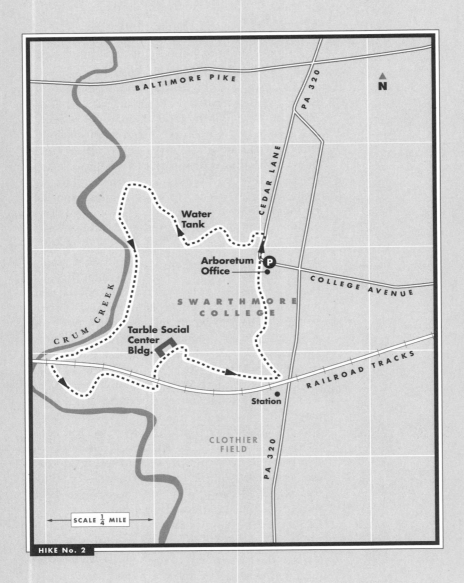

BALTIMORE PIKE

PA 320

N

CEDAR LANE

Water
Tank

Arboretum
Office

P

COLLEGE AVENUE

SWARTHMORE
COLLEGE

CRUM CREEK

Tarble Social
Center
Bldg.

RAILROAD TRACKS

Station

CLOTHIER
FIELD

PA 320

SCALE ¼ MILE

HIKE No. 2

No. 2

Scott Arboretum

Swarthmore College
500 College Avenue
Swarthmore, PA 19081
(610) 328-8025

Distance	2.0 miles
Elevation	270 feet
Time to hike	1 hour
Surface	asphalt path through the campus; woods trail through the natural areas of the park, along Crum Creek
Interesting features	over 5,000 different kinds of plants that grow in the Delaware Valley
Facilities	many benches, even a swing from a tree; water fountains; no rest rooms or picnic facilities
Disability access	yes, on the asphalt path; however, the uncultivated parts of the campus (along Crum Creek) are not accessible to wheeled hikers
Hunting	no

Directions **from I-476 (Blue Route) near Media:**

1. take exit 2 (Swarthmore), drive east on Baltimore Pike for 0.7 mile
2. turn right (south) onto PA 320, drive 0.6 mile
3. at second light, turn right onto College Avenue, onto the campus
4. proceed one block to the Scott office and parking lot on the left

Coordinates 39°54'23"N; 75°21'06"W

The Scott Arboretum is on the campus of, and creates the landscape for, Swarthmore College, a coeducational college of 1,300 students located 11 miles southwest of Philadelphia. The arboretum grows more than 5,000 different kinds of plants particular to the Delaware Valley on the 330-acre campus. The trees, shrubs, and perennials are selected for their ease of maintenance and disease resistance in this area, as well as their ornamental qualities. The plants are labeled with both their common and scientific names, and similar plants are grouped in collections, making this hike a good opportunity to learn identification of species. A brochure, with guide map, is available at the arboretum office on College Avenue. Helpful arboretum guides can also help you plan a walk to see particular plants in bloom at various times of the year. The arboretum office is open Monday through Friday, from 8:30 a.m. to 4:30 p.m.

Major collections include flowering cherries, crabapples, lilacs, azaleas, magnolias, rhododendrons, tree peonies, viburnums, wisteria, and witch hazels. In addition, there are specialty gardens featuring spring flowering shrubs and plants, a rose garden, a fragrance garden, a winter garden, and a holly collection. April or May is a wonderful time to visit the arboretum, and the following one-hour hike will take you past most of the spring-blooming plants, as well as the natural or uncultivated parts of the arboretum along Crum Creek.

Park at the small parking lot adjacent to the arboretum office. Begin by crossing College Avenue at Cedar Lane. Just to the left is a large map of the entire campus. Along Cedar Lane, you pass many varieties of flowering cherries on the left. Under the cherry trees the rhododendrons and azaleas bloom, along with the daffodils, hyacinths, and tulips of spring.

Turn left at the asphalt path, and walk past broad sweeping lawns bordered by more rhododendrons and azaleas. Turn right and walk around the Friends Meeting House, surrounded by flowering pink and white dogwoods. Cross Whittier Place and turn left on the asphalt walkway. Stately oaks and spring flowering viburnums and hydrangeas line the road. At the corner is the DuPont Science Building. Continue straight ahead to visit the Harry Wood Memorial Garden, located in the courtyard. This garden includes evergreens and deciduous plants, with various species in bloom at various times of the year. From here, wheelchair hikers may continue on accessible, smooth pathways to the rest of the campus.

To visit the uncultivated part of the campus, turn right on the walkway and continue past the water tower at a sign indicating the "Swarthmore College Conservation Area" on a woods trail. The trail leads steeply downhill through a mature oak and beech forest, to Crum Creek. Turn left on the trail to walk along the creek. At 0.7 mile, you ascend the steep slope through hemlocks and rhododendrons along the well-defined trail. Cross under the railroad trestle bridge at 1.0 mile. Crum Meadow, on the right, is bordered by a collection of more than 200 varieties of deciduous and evergreen hollies. Follow the trail and turn left on an old gravel road.

At the top of a hill you reenter the more cultivated section of the campus. Turn left at the road, and cross back over the railroad tracks on a bridge. On the right side are tennis courts. Straight ahead is the Tarble Social Center building, surrounded by native azaleas. In the courtyard of the building is the fragrance garden, with trees, perennials, annuals, and bulbs grown for their fragrant flowers or foliage.

Just past the tennis courts turn right at a very large tree—a bender oak, a hybrid oak. Walk past

large saucer magnolias in bloom. Just ahead is
Magill Walk, lined with large oaks. Turn left toward
Parrish Hall, the main administration building.
Just before the steps, turn right on another
walkway, then left at Willets dormitory, behind the
arboretum office. Behind the office is the Terry
Shane Teaching Garden, which highlights the
major plant collections of the arboretum in a garden setting. Here you will find benches, a grape
arbor, and a fountain. Walk around the building
to return to the parking lot and your car.

Springfield Trail No.3

For information only **Springfield Trail Club**
5121 Pontiac Road
Drexel Hill, PA 19026

Distance	4.5 miles
Elevation	260 feet
Time to hike	2 hours
Surface	woods trail; short sections along SEPTA (Southeastern Pennsylvania Transportation Authority) tracks and sidewalks
Interesting features	hike on uncultivated terrain near suburban development; garnets are sometimes found along Whiskey Run and Crum Creek
Facilities	water, rest rooms, picnic tables at Smedley Park
Disability access	no
Hunting	no

Directions **from I-476 (Blue Route) near Media:**

1. take exit 2 (Swarthmore), drive east on Baltimore Pike for 0.7 mile
2. turn left (north) onto PA 320, drive 1.5 miles
3. turn right (south) on PA 420 (Woodland Avenue)
4. turn left immediately into shopping center parking lot

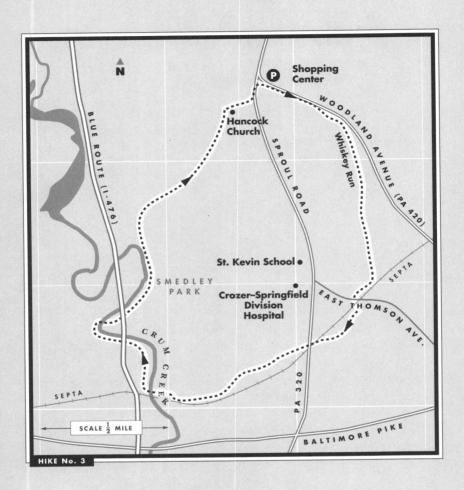

N

Shopping
Center

WOODLAND AVENUE (PA 420)

Hancock
Church

SPROUL ROAD

Whiskey Run

BLUE ROUTE (I-476)

St. Kevin School ●

SMEDLEY
PARK

Crozer–Springfield
Division
Hospital

SEPTA

EAST THOMSON AVE.

CRUM CREEK

PA 320

SEPTA

SCALE ½ MILE

BALTIMORE PIKE

HIKE No. 3

This hike was developed through the cooperative efforts of Springfield Township and private property owners in 1969, and it is maintained by the Springfield Trail Club. It is an example of a natural woodland trail right in the midst of suburban development. Although never very far from civilization, it does have a remote feeling in many places. The trail, which has had to be slightly relocated because of the construction of the nearby Blue Route, is regularly maintained and should be fairly easy to follow. However, in the fall the yellow blazes can be difficult to distinguish from the leaves of the many birch and sassafras along the trail. Watch especially carefully for the double blazes indicating turns.

From the parking lot, carefully cross PA 420 at the light and turn left to walk southeast on the sidewalk along Woodland Avenue. At 0.2 mile cross James Lane and turn right, just before the Kovacs Funeral Home. Watch for the yellow blazes that signal a turn left into the woods, just before you reach a house. The yellow blazes lead downhill toward Whiskey Run through Spring Valley Park, a local township park. You will cross Whiskey Run several times on stepping stones.

After passing the E.T. Richardson Middle School on your left, at 1.0 mile you will reach the SEPTA trolley tracks. Turn right to walk along the tracks. The yellow blazes are painted on the concrete supports for the overhead lines. Do not walk on the tracks!

At East Thomson Avenue, turn left and cross the tracks to Stidman Drive. Turn right on Stidman, a short access road for an apartment parking lot. The blazes are painted on guardrail posts on the left side of the road. Near the end of the parking lot, follow the blazes to climb over and down a 4-foot-high stone wall at 1.1 miles.

You continue through second-growth woods with the tracks at some distance. Cross the tracks again at 1.5 miles. From here, you walk beside the tracks under the Sproul Road (PA 320) bridge, then sharply down a steep embankment to cross Whiskey Run. At 1.7 miles you will see the Springfield Shopping Center off to your left. This is an area of overgrown meadow, with the narrow trail passing through brambles and vines.

At 2.2 miles you will come to the tracks again. Walk along them for only about 30 feet, then turn right, uphill, for a fairly steep climb to a point overlooking the tracks. Descend to Paper Mill Road and Smedley Park at 2.3 miles. Follow the rock grit path past playground equipment and cross a metal footbridge over Crum Creek. Then follow the blazes on an old woods road. This is the most remote section of the hike, and you will see many large mature sycamores, beeches, and tuliptrees.

The trail follows the woods road, leaves it briefly along Crum Creek, and then returns to it before reaching the massive concrete pillars supporting the Blue Route, which was completed in 1992. At 2.7 miles you are actually under the Blue Route. The trail makes a loop on the other side of the Blue Route, then circles underneath it again. Continue on the gravel road, but watch carefully for the double yellow blazes, which indicate a turn to the left to reenter the woods.

From here, the trail parallels Crum Creek about 100 feet above it, then descends to an unnamed tributary at 3.5 miles. The trail is frequently rocky, as it crosses and recrosses the little stream many times.

Despite their proximity to homes, roads, and other signs of human habitation, deer, raccoon, turkey, and fox live in these woods. Look for their tracks in the mud along the little stream and along Whiskey Run. See the illustrations below for help in identifying their tracks.

Notice the massive rock outcroppings, as you gradually climb out of the ravine. A sign placed by Springfield Township warns of the danger of falling rocks.

At 4.0 miles you cross a bridge to Lownes Park, with a playground and basketball courts, right to the edge of the woods. However, watch for the yellow blazes on the left and stay on the trail as it continues to follow the now-tiny creek. At 4.8 miles you reach the top of the ravine and come out of the woods onto the grassy lawn of Hancock United Methodist Church. Walk along the row of evergreens shrubs, cross PA 320 (Sproul Road), then PA 420 (Woodland Avenue) to return to your car.

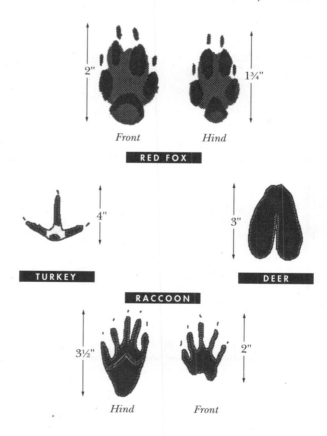

2" 1¾"

Front   Hind

RED FOX

4"   3"

TURKEY   DEER

RACCOON

3½"   2"

Hind   Front

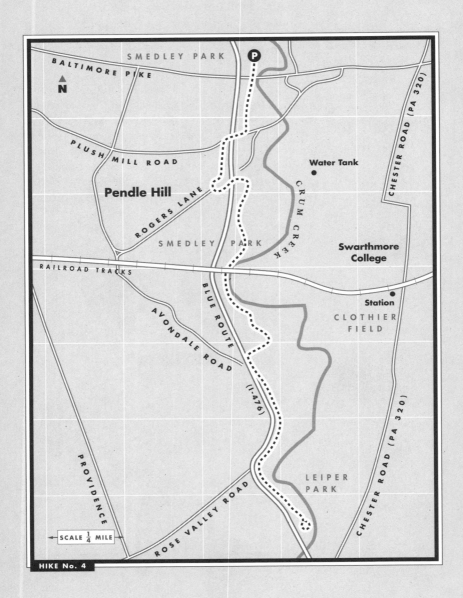

SMEDLEY PARK

BALTIMORE PIKE

N

PLUSH MILL ROAD

Pendle Hill

ROGERS LANE

SMEDLEY PARK

Water Tank

CRUM CREEK

CHESTER ROAD (PA 320)

Swarthmore College

RAILROAD TRACKS

BLUE ROUTE

AVONDALE ROAD

(I-476)

Station

CLOTHIER FIELD

PROVIDENCE

SCALE ¼ MILE

ROSE VALLEY ROAD

LEIPER PARK

CHESTER ROAD (PA 320)

HIKE No. 4

Leiper–Smedley Trail

For information only **Nether Providence Township Building**
214 Sykes Lane
Wallingford, PA 19085
(610) 566-4516

Distance	4.0 miles
Elevation	80 feet
Time to hike	2 hours
Surface	6-foot-wide paved surface
Interesting features	passes over, under, and along the Blue Route and Crum Creek; natural settings and wildlife in the midst of suburban development; new environmental education center at Smedley Park; Leiper House (circa 1785) at Avondale Road
Facilities	rest rooms, water, and picnic tables at Smedley Park and Leiper Park
Disability access	yes, start to finish; Thomas Leiper House, not accessible
Hunting	no

Directions **from I-476 (Blue Route) near Media:**

1. take exit 2 (Swarthmore), drive east on Baltimore Pike for 0.3 mile
2. turn left onto Paper Mill Road, drive 0.2 mile
3. turn left, following signs to the visitors' center at Smedley Park

The Leiper–Smedley Trail, also known as the Blue Route Trail, was completed along with the highway in 1992. Ninety percent of the cost of the construction of the trail was paid for by federal highway dollars; the rest was funded by Delaware County and Nether Providence Township. The trail has a definite suburban flavor, never very far from housing development and the highway. However, you may be surprised by the variety of habitats and wildlife to be found. Park at the new environmental education center at Smedley Park, operated by Delaware County and the Penn State Cooperative Extension Service. At the end of the parking lot you will find the signs for the Leiper–Smedley Trail.

At 0.1 mile, you round a turn down a slight grade to busy Baltimore Pike. There is a yellow button to control the traffic light to allow a safe crossing. Continuing with the Blue Route on your right, you reach Plush Mill Road at 0.3 mile. Here you turn right to cross over the Blue Route. Just ahead is the Community Arts Center, the largest nonprofit center for the arts in Delaware County. Classes in arts and crafts, concerts, exhibitions, and a summer art camp are offered here.

Turn left, following the signs. There are noise barrier fences and 5-foot chain link fencing on the left, with a mix of grass and second-growth woodlands on the right. At 0.8 mile you reach Pendle Hill and Rogers Lane, and cross the Blue Route again. This section has many mature oaks and other hardwoods, with pachysandra and English ivy growing on the ground to your left. At 1.0 mile walk under a railroad bridge, which continues as a trestle across the deep gorge of Crum Creek.

At 1.1 miles you will reach a rest area, with two benches facing the Blue Route. Here you can watch the traffic whizzing by, beneath the shade of basswood, American elm, yellow-poplar, and sugar maple trees. Behind you through dense woods and across

Crum Creek is the Swarthmore College campus. A few steps farther on along the trail you will come to the remains of a large estate, including the ruins of an Italian water garden. Pools, fountains, stone walls, and steps are largely overtaken by vegetation.

Paths that lead off to the left through the woods go to the Swarthmore campus. Continue straight ahead on the main trail past a grassy area and a holding pond for water runoff from the Blue Route. Low shrubs and meadow provide rich habitat for songbirds. Continue down a short hill and cross Crum Creek on a wooden footbridge directly under the highway at 1.5 miles. Cross Avondale Road, turning left on the sidewalk. Steep concrete steps on the right lead up to a parking area. Continue straight ahead under the Blue Route along Avondale Road.

You emerge from under the highway. To the right is a 100-foot-wide grassy strip between Avondale Road and the Blue Route. Here we spotted a red fox with a cub who had made her home in a culvert adjacent to an oil pipeline junction station. The fox reluctantly trotted away from her cub, hidden in the culvert, glancing back anxiously at us while she crossed Avondale Road and circled back along Crum Creek on the other side.

Continue ahead and cross Rose Valley Road at 1.8 miles. Follow the sign to the Leiper House, which is 0.3 mile ahead on Avondale Road. Thomas Leiper owned an extensive milling and stone quarrying business here along Crum Creek, supporting an industrial village from 1780 to 1940. Leiper Park has tables and benches and is a tranquil setting for picnics or fishing along Crum Creek. The house and four outbuildings were built in 1785 and overlook the park. The Leiper House, furnished with antiques dating from around 1800, is open Saturdays and Sundays from 1:00 to 4:00 p.m. except in January, February, and March; a small donation is requested for a tour. At Leiper Park you will turn and retrace your route to return to Smedley Park and your car, for a total hike of 4.0 miles.

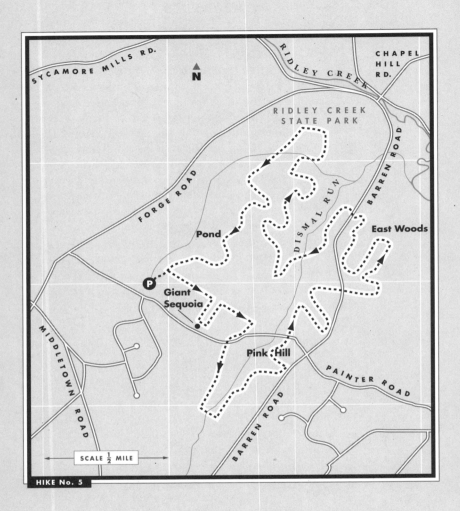

SYCAMORE MILLS RD.

N

RIDLEY CREEK

CHAPEL
HILL
RD.

RIDLEY CREEK
STATE PARK

FORGE ROAD

BARREN ROAD

Pond

DISMAL RUN

East Woods

P

Giant
Sequoia

Pink Hill

MIDDLETOWN ROAD

PAINTER ROAD

BARREN ROAD

SCALE ½ MILE

HIKE No. 5

Tyler Arboretum No. 5

515 Painter Road
Media, PA 19063
(610) 566-5431

Distance	10.5 miles
Elevation	800 feet
Time to hike	4½ hours
Surface	grassy lawns; mown path through meadow; woods trail; woods road
Interesting features	large variety of native and exotic trees; collections of rhododendrons and azaleas; remnants of serpentine barren (Pink Hill); Dismal Run and Rocky Run; specialty gardens—fragrant, butterfly, and bird; 700-acre arboretum; 200 cultivated acres and 500 acres of natural woodland, meadow, and marsh
Facilities	water, rest rooms at visitors' center; many benches; picnicking only at parking lot
Disability access	no
Hunting	no

1. take PA 252 north for 0.5 mile to Providence Road (SR 4001), turn left
2. drive 1.1 miles to Chapel Hill Road, turn left
3. drive 0.5 mile to bridge over Ridley Creek— proceed straight ahead on Barren Road (SR 4004)
4. drive 1.2 miles, turn right onto Painter Road
5. drive 1.0 mile—the entrance to the arboretum and the parking lot are on the right

Coordinates 39°56'06"N; 75°26'32"W

The Tyler Arboretum was created by Minshall and Jacob Painter, bachelor Quaker brothers, who from 1849 to 1876 planted almost a thousand species of shrubs and trees on their 300-acre family estate. The grounds were expanded and further developed by John J. Tyler, a nephew, and in 1945 the estate became a public arboretum. Funding is from the Tyler trust, private donations, and memberships, as well as from admissions charged for educational programs. There is an admission fee (adults: $3.00; children 3–15: $1.00; children under 3: free) to visit the arboretum.

There are 20 miles of trails throughout the 700-acre arboretum. The white-blazed Wilderness Trail takes the hiker through the major cultivated collections, remains of stone farm structures from the 1800s, natural features such as remnants of a serpentine barren on Pink Hill, as well as isolated scenic areas of streams and woodlands.

From the parking lot your first stop is the large stone barn that houses the visitors' center and bookstore, where you can obtain a map and other information. Circle around the barn to the wide park-like lawn, with labeled specimen trees, many planted by the Painter brothers in the mid-1800s.

Notice in particular an Oriental spruce with drooping branches that stands more than 100 feet high, a Yulan magnolia from central China, a rare cedar-of-Lebanon from Syria, a Chinese multi-trunked ginkgo, a yellow buckeye, a 100-foot baldcypress, a giant tuliptree, river birches, and English elms.

Walk down the sloping lawn to a wooden footbridge, which is the start of four blazed trails. Bear left for 50 feet to the sign for three additional trails, including the Wilderness Trail. This trail is clearly marked with white blazes but can be difficult to follow where other trails intersect. Watch carefully for the double blazes indicating a turn.

The trail leads past hemlocks, spruces, and a collection of large hybrid rhododendrons, which bloom in May in colors from white to pink to red.

At 0.7 mile you reach the oldest giant sequoia tree in the eastern United States, planted in 1859. This tree stands 65 feet high. Notice the double trunk near the top. Forty years after the tree was planted, somebody cut off the top for a Christmas tree!

Continue following the white blazes to the 25-acre Pinetum, including rows of pine, spruce, hemlock, and cedar. Adjacent is an open field area that attracts and holds as many as fifty bluebird pairs all year long.

The trail enters the uncultivated natural woods and crosses Painter Road at 1.4 miles. Shrubs and dense thickets provide good cover for a variety of songbirds on abandoned farmland. At 1.5 miles you reach the remains of an old farm, including a magnificent arched stone barn, a farmhouse, and a springhouse, overgrown with honeysuckle, wild rose, and sumac. At 1.6 miles, jump over Dismal Run. Here beech trees predominate.

The Wilderness Trail is not well maintained in the Pink Hill and East Woods areas, which lie ahead, and the trail is sometimes indistinct, especially in fall when leaves cover the trail. Watch carefully for the blazes, especially the double blazes indicating a turn.

At 2.9 miles, after a steady climb, you reach Pink Hill, named for the moss pink that bloom in May. The serpentine soil, which has a distinct greenish cast, is shallow and toxic to most plants. However, shrubs, aspens, birches, and unusual wildflowers flourish in these open meadows, which cannot support other vegetation.

At 3.3 miles cross Painter Road again. Continue through mixed hardwood forest, following the trail as it crosses Barren Road at 4.1 miles to enter East Woods. At 5.4 miles watch on the left for a post with a circular disc on the top. An arrow can be rotated to point to examples of eight tree species commonly found in these woods—yellow-poplar or tuliptree, hickory, black gum, red maple, white oak, red oak, chestnut oak, beech. At 6.3 miles the trail crosses Barren Road again.

At 6.9 miles you reach Dismal Run and the site of a Delaware County cooperative fish nursery project. Medium-size trout are protected within a diverted 60-foot section of the stream in wire enclosures. Cross Dismal Run on a wooden footbridge. After several hundred feet you come to the remains of a massive stone fireplace, which is what is left of an abandoned farmhouse. The trail climbs steadily uphill, then descends to Rocky Run at 8.0 miles. Indian Rock, at the base of an old yellow- poplar, is 30 feet downstream. Cross Rocky Run on stepping stones. The trail ascends again to level walking; a pine plantation in Ridley Creek State Park is on your right. At 9.5 miles, cross Rocky Run again.

Several other trails now run with the white-blazed trail. Again you are on abandoned farmland. You are very likely to spot deer near an old apple orchard. Wire fences 5 feet high have been erected to keep the deer away from the nearby cultivated plants, with limited success. Note several catalpa trees with their distinctive, very large leaves. At 10.0 miles the trail passes through an area with large, cultivated azaleas, hollies, and yellow-poplars. Pass a small pond on the right at 10.1 miles. The pond was built around 1950 to provide irrigation water to the rhododendron collections being planted uphill. Toads and frogs breed in the pond, and you will also find waterlilies and wildflowers along the banks.

At 10.2 miles cross the wooden bridge again and the wide lawn to the visitors' center. Adjacent to the center are the aptly named fragrant, butterfly, and bird gardens. Surrounding the parking lot are magnolias, lilacs, and flowering cherries, spectacular when they bloom in spring. Return to your car at 10.5 miles.

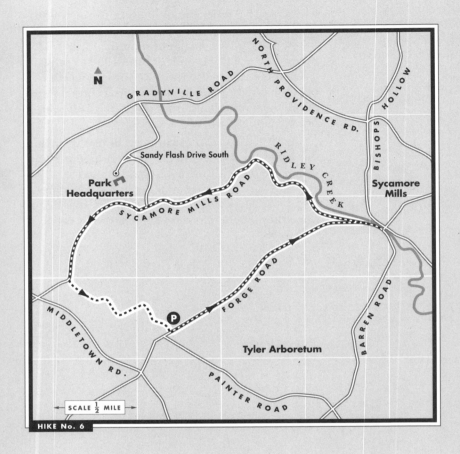

N

GRADYVILLE ROAD

NORTH PROVIDENCE RD.

BISHOPS HOLLOW

Sandy Flash Drive South

RIDLEY CREEK

Park
Headquarters

Sycamore
Mills

SYCAMORE MILLS ROAD

FORGE ROAD

P

MIDDLETOWN RD.

BARREN ROAD

Tyler Arboretum

PAINTER ROAD

SCALE ½ MILE

HIKE No. 6

Ridley Creek

No. 6

Ridley Creek State Park

Sycamore Mills Road
Media, PA 19063-4398
(610) 892-3900

Distance	5.0 miles
Elevation	260 feet
Time to hike	2½ hours
Surface	paved roads and asphalt path closed to vehicles
Interesting features	various stages of forest regeneration; Sycamore Mills, a colonial village, consisting of ruins of a gristmill, sawmill, and residences; a pine plantation; varied habitats of meadow, thicket, and hardwood forest
Facilities	several portable toilets along trail; water at visitors' center; picnic tables with grills; many benches along trail
Disability access	yes; the multi-use trail described (Forge Road–Sycamore Mills Road–paved path) is a paved loop for use by wheelchairs and bikes but not by motor vehicles
Hunting	no, except for posted deer hunts to control the deer population

1. take PA 252 north for 0.5 mile to Providence Road (SR 4001), turn left

2. drive on Providence Road for 2.4 miles

3. turn left onto Gradyville Road, drive 1.1 miles

4. bear left on Sandy Flash Drive South, drive 1.5 miles

5. turn right to follow the signs to parking area number 15

Coordinates   39°56'39"N; 75°27'22"W

Ridley Creek State Park contains 12 miles of hiking trails, through woodlands, meadows, and farmland reverting to forest. This hike as described includes these habitats, as well as Sycamore Mills, a colonial village. It is entirely on a paved path and is accessible to hikers and bicyclists. Pick up a trail map at the park headquarters on Sandy Flash Drive South as you drive in. You will notice that many of the trees are numbered along Ridley Creek. The numbers refer to a 48-item tree-identification quiz; you can also pick up an answer key at the park office.

The 5-mile multi-use loop trail can be accessed at several points. It is accessible to the wheelchair hiker at the parking lot near the Sycamore Mills bridge, or at parking area number15, as described here. Begin the hike by following the asphalt trail west of the parking lot, past a yellow gate.

Turn left onto Forge Road. On busy weekends be sure to observe the sign instructing walkers and joggers to stay to the left on the trail. Bicycles pass on the right. Forge Road is adjacent to the Tyler Arboretum and a large pine plantation on the right. On the left are several fields in various stages of succession—meadows gradually being overtaken by saplings and thickets of multiflora rose and honeysuckle. Although May is the peak month for forest wildflowers, meadow and field wildflowers bloom later and throughout the summer. Thick brush and thicket provide cover to a large bird population of chirpy thrushes and warblers.

Continue steeply downhill past a large black oak on the right, then a shagbark hickory tree on the left to Ridley Creek at 1.3 miles. Large beeches and yellow-poplars or tuliptrees, birches, sycamores, and ferns predominate along the stream. Turn right, onto Sycamore Mills Road, which leads to Sycamore Mills.

Sycamore Mills is the site of what was once a thriving industrial colonial village. A gristmill was built here in 1718, used by area farmers for grinding grain, including wheat, rye, barley, and corn. The gristmill was the economic base of the community. A sawmill was built thirty years later, and it operated only when the gristmill was idle. It was a sister industry to the gristmill, providing lumber for a growing construction business. The sawmill and gristmill occupied the flat area across the stream, just below the mill dam. Both were destroyed by a fire in 1901; only the mill dam remains. Blacksmith and wheelwright shops, the mill office and library, the mill owner's residence, a nail factory, a stone springhouse, a rolling and slitting mill, a community bakehouse, and workers' cottages completed the village. Several of these eighteenth-century structures are now leased as residences; foundations and ruins remain of others. Continue to the Sycamore Mills bridge and parking lot at 1.6 miles. From here, you will turn back to retrace your steps.

Return along Ridley Creek on Sycamore Mills Road. At 2.5 miles a gravel road leads 150 feet to the stream and a handicapped-accessible fishing platform. It is located in a prime fishing section for trout, at a bend in the creek containing deep water and large boulders.

At 2.6 miles the road turns to the left away from the creek. As you gradually climb, the sycamore and beech trees give way to white and red oak, hickory, and black walnut trees. At 3.4 miles a gravel path leads over a bridge to the park office (this trail is not wheelchair accessible). The office is located in the "Hunting Hill" mansion, built by the Jeffords family in 1914. The area west of the mansion contains formal gardens, plantings, and fountains.

Continue on Sycamore Mills Road to a paved path at 4.2 miles and turn left. Overgrown meadows on both sides provide cover for songbirds. Raspberries and blackberries ripen here in July. Continue to Forge Road at 5.0 miles, and turn left to return to the parking lot and your car.

For a side trip within Ridley Creek State Park: In the northern portion of the park, on Sandy Flash Drive North, is a colonial Pennsylvania plantation. The plantation has been a working farm for more than 300 years, and it gives an accurate picture of what life was like on a typical Quaker farm before the American Revolution. It is restored to its late eighteenth-century appearance, complete with animals typical of the period and authentically dressed historical interpreters. A small fee is charged to visitors ($3.00 for adults; $1.50 for children 4–12 and senior citizens).

No 7

Schuylkill Center for Environmental Education

8480 Hagys Mill Road
Philadelphia, PA 19128-9976
(215) 482-7300

Distance	2.8 miles
Elevation	290 feet
Time to hike	1½ hours
Surface	grassy woods road; woods trails
Interesting features	7 miles of trails through various animal habitats; four ponds; a wetlands area; exhibits of interest to children
Facilities	water, rest rooms, and picnic tables at visitors' center; many benches along trails and beside ponds
Disability access	the visitors' center and the quarter-mile Widener Trail wheelchair accessible; otherwise, no
Hunting	no

Directions **from I-476 (Blue Route) near Conshohocken:**

1. take exit 7, at Conshohocken, drive east on Ridge Pike 3.7 miles

2. turn right onto Spring Lane (at Texaco station), drive 0.6 mile

3. turn left onto Hagys Mill Road, drive 0.3 mile and turn right onto gravel road

4. continue 0.6 mile to the Schuylkill Environmental Education Center

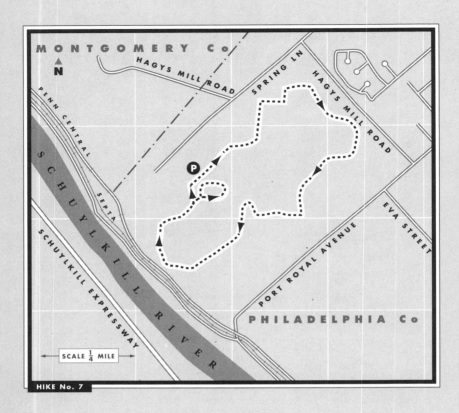

Coordinates   40°03'38"N; 75°14'42"W

The Schuylkill Center is the largest (500 acres) privately owned natural area within the city of Philadelphia, with 7 miles of hiking trails, four ponds, a wetlands area, and bird blinds. It also has a wildlife rehabilitation center that annually treats 3,000 ill, injured, and orphaned wild animals.

The Schuylkill Environmental Education Center features hands-on exhibits for elementary school children, including a microscope to see tiny animals, a terrarium with turtles and snakes, an observation beehive, a fish tank, a weather station, and a sandbox to make and learn about animal tracks. The center and trails are open Monday through Saturday 8:30 a.m. to 4:30 p.m.; and Sunday 1:00 to 4:30 p.m. There is an admission fee of $5.00 for adults, $3.00 for children (2–12 years).

Begin your hike at the visitors' center, where you can pick up a trail map.

The Widener Trail starts to the left of the center as you face the entrance. It is paved and passes a small pond with a wooden deck and seats. The trail ends at 0.25 mile at a bird blind with feeders that are kept filled all year.

At the bird blind, turn left on the Gray Fox Loop. This trail gently slopes up and down for 0.9 mile, through fields and wooded areas. You pass Founders' Grove, a memorial tree collection that is fenced to protect it from the many deer. The trail takes you through a pine plantation and old farmland reverting to forest, and it ends at Wind Dance Pond.

Wind Dance Pond Trail takes you around the small pond, with mallard and other ducks and Canada geese. Great blue herons and the smaller green herons also frequently visit in spring, summer, and fall. The trail continues through a stand of beech trees.

You will pass an old stone springhouse over a wooden footbridge to pick up the Ravine Loop Trail. At 1.5 miles cross a 60-foot impoundment on a boardwalk; the water is crystal clear to the bottom. The Ravine Trail passes through a stream-fed marshy area, then narrows to a steep ravine, crossing and recrossing a small stream. The trail is steep but smooth. Rock outcroppings shine with mica, schist, quartzite, and sometimes garnets. After a rather steep uphill climb, you pass two small artificial ponds with small docks, bird feeding stations, and benches. In this area we spotted two groups of four deer, which were quite tame. We were able to slowly approach to within 30 feet of one group.

From here, leave the Ravine Trail onto the Towhee and Cattail trails past another bird blind and bird feeding station. The trail loops back to return to the Ravine Trail. You will return to the visitors' center and your car via the Upper Field Trail. From the Upper Field Trail overlooking a meadow you have a spectacular view of center-city Philadelphia from a very secluded and tranquil location.

No.8

Andorra Natural Area

Northwestern Avenue
Philadelphia, PA 19118
(215) 685-9285

Distance	2.5 miles
Elevation	240 feet
Time to hike	1½ hours
Surface	grassy two-track road; paths through woods and meadows
Interesting features	once part of the Andorra nursery, which was the largest nursery on the East Coast; labeled trees, many very old—paper birch (over 90 years), white oak (300 years), cucumbertree (250 years), "The Great Beech," and giant scarlet, black, and white oaks; programs for children and adults, including bird walks, family scavenger hunts, and other programs (all free)
Facilities	water and picnic tables at Tree House; inquire at Tree House for directions to rest rooms (at nearby stables); benches along trails
Disability access	no
Hunting	no

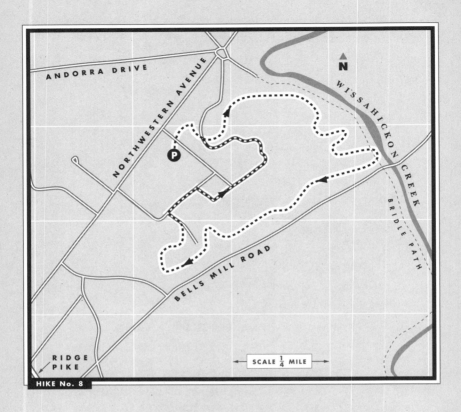

ANDORRA DRIVE

NORTHWESTERN AVENUE

N

WISSAHICKON CREEK

BRIDLE PATH

P

BELLS MILL ROAD

RIDGE
PIKE

SCALE ¼ MILE

HIKE No. 8

1. take exit 7 at Conshohocken, drive east on Ridge Pike for 3.5 miles to Northwestern Avenue

2. turn left (at Friendly's Restaurant) onto Northwestern Avenue (a narrow 1½ lane road), drive 0.6 mile

3. turn right into upper parking lot, follow signs to the Tree House Visitor Center

Coordinates   40°04'49"N; 75°14'08"W

Andorra Natural Area is heavily wooded, roughly square, about 0.5 mile on each side. It is part of Fairmount Park but is fairly isolated, and it does not receive as many visitors as more well-known areas of the park.

Begin at the Tree House, where you climb outdoor steps to a second-floor porch. Pick up a well-drawn, accurate map at the Tree House Visitor Center on the porch. The visitors' center is open weekends in spring, summer, and fall. If it is open, step inside for additional materials as well as exhibits and artifacts. Guides at the center can tell you about recent sightings of birds and animals.

From the Tree House, begin walking east on the E. Smith Trail, just beyond the gate in front of the Tree House. Follow the sign to the Azalea Loop, past a bird blind and through a natural tulip meadow. Pass a grove of large paper birch trees. From here, pick up the Ginger Trail, which parallels the Wissahickon Carriage Road (closed to vehicles) and Wissahickon Creek.

At the top of a rise, where you will enjoy a view that gives no hint of civilization nearby, the trail intersects with the Secret Valley Trail. Follow it steeply downhill to the Wissahickon Creek and the eastern corner of the park. Just before Bells Mill

Road, look for the Bells Mill Trail, which parallels the road going west. Pass a large bamboo field on the right. Bamboo, native to the Orient, was brought to Philadelphia as an ornamental in the 1800s and now thrives in several locations. The foliage dies in the winter and turns brown, only to grow and flourish in the summer; the plants grow to ten feet and more.

Just after the trail turns away from Bells Mill Road, there is a very large yellow-poplar tree, 330 years old. This marks the start of the appropriately named Big Tree Trail. Many, although not all, trail intersections are marked with signs. Cross over an intermittent stream; follow the trail as it again parallels Bells Mill Road for a short distance before turning north.

You will pass the remains of Black Farm on your right, an abandoned farm reverting to meadow and small trees. Turn left at a grassy two-track, Honeysuckle Road, through blackberry fields and a meadow. These fields contain many saplings and wildflowers and are alive with birds. Turn right at Deer Yard Trail, proceed to Beech Row Trail, and turn right again, where you find a magnificent grove of American beech trees. Little grows beneath the dense shade of these huge trees.

As you return to the Tree House on the well-marked Nursery Trail, you will find other more exotic tree varieties, such as Chinese cedrela, Japanese cryptomeria, and Japanese falsecypress. These trees were planted in the 1800s, and each is clearly labeled.

Explanatory signs along the trails describe the plants, natural history, and wildlife found in the park. There are bird feeding stations, blinds, and a salt lick to attract deer, which are plentiful. Andorra is a lovely, unspoiled natural area, where it is possible to spend an entire afternoon and hardly notice you are within the city limits of Philadelphia.

Wissahickon Gorge

No.9

For information only   **Friends of the Wissahickon**

8708 Germantown Avenue
Philadelphia, PA 19118
(215) 247-0417

Distance	9.2 miles
Elevation	180 feet
Time to hike	4½ hours
Surface	hard-packed rock grit (Forbidden Drive); woods trail
Interesting features	deep, hemlock-filled gorge; geologic formations; historic bridges and buildings
Facilities	benches, picnic facilities along Forbidden Drive; public water and rest rooms at Valley Green
Disability access	yes, on Forbidden Drive; otherwise, no
Hunting	no

Directions   **from I-476 (Blue Route) near Conshohocken:**

1. take exit 7 at Conshohocken, drive east on Ridge Pike for 3.7 miles to Bells Mill Road
2. turn left on Bells Mill Road for 0.9 mile, park at parking lot on the right

Coordinates   40°04'42"N; 75°13'39"W

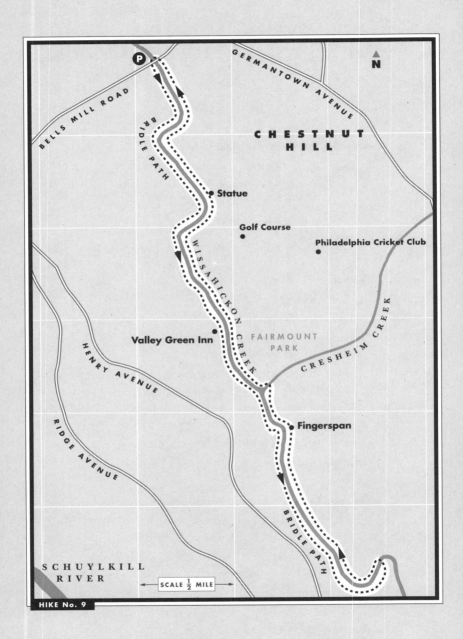

P

N

GERMANTOWN AVENUE

BELLS MILL ROAD

BRIDLE PATH

CHESTNUT
HILL

● Statue

Golf Course
●

Philadelphia Cricket Club
●

WISSAHICKON CREEK

CRESHEIM CREEK

FAIRMOUNT
PARK

HENRY AVENUE

Valley Green Inn
●

● Fingerspan

RIDGE AVENUE

BRIDLE PATH

SCHUYLKILL
RIVER

← SCALE ½ MILE →

HIKE No. 9

Wissahickon Creek, as it carves its way to the Schuylkill River, has been a favorite place for promenades since it was acquired for Fairmount Park in 1868. Dramatic scenery, consisting of mature stands of hemlock and rhododendron, rocky outcroppings, and the creek itself provide a real wilderness feeling within the city of Philadelphia. This circuit hike connects a wide bridle path (Forbidden Drive) on the west side of the creek with the much more rugged Wissahickon Gorge Trail on the east side.

From the end of the parking lot, walk down the trail to Forbidden (or Wissahickon) Drive. This wide carriage road is used by bicyclists, runners, joggers, horseback riders, and parents pushing baby strollers and is closed to motor vehicles, except for a very short section from Wises Mill Road to the Valley Green Inn. It is accessible for wheelchair hikers. Turn right to walk along the creek. Walking along the carriage road, you pass three arched stone bridges, at 1.0, 2.1, and 2.7 miles; the hike can be shortened by crossing at any of them and returning on the orange-blazed Wissahickon Gorge Trail.

At 0.6 mile you pass a covered bridge, a 1939 restoration of the original bridge that was built in 1737. Stop at the next bench facing the creek. Just opposite this bench, high up and overlooking the creek, is a statue of a kneeling Lenape warrior, Tedyuscung, carved in 1902.

The Lenapes were the original settlers of the Wissahickon. The name "Wissahickon" is derived from either the Indian word wisamikon, meaning "catfish stream," or wissauchsickan, meaning "yellow-colored stream." The creek was historically a good place for catfish, and it still provides good fishing. You will also see several species of ducks, Canada geese, and an occasional egret. We even saw a couple of deer swimming across the creek.

During the eighteenth and early nineteenth centuries the Wissahickon was an important industrial center. The creek, falling 100 feet in 7 miles, provided the power for grist-, saw-, and papermills, as well as for canneries. You will notice the remains of stone buildings and dams on both sides of the creek. The area was acquired by the Fairmount Park Commission in 1868, originally to protect the purity of Philadelphia's water supply. The manufacturing industry ended, and shortly afterward the mills were torn down.

In the mid-nineteenth century there were dozens of roadhouses and taverns bordering Wissahickon Creek and the Schuylkill River. The Valley Green Inn at 2.1 miles, built in 1850, is the only establishment remaining in operation. Inside are displayed early American tools, glassware, and paintings depicting life along the Wissahickon.

At 4.4 miles, at a bend in the creek and just after an old stone building on the left, cross the creek on a wooden footbridge. The narrow woods trail, as it runs up and down the hillside, is of a much different character than the carriage road. It will probably take longer by a half hour or more to return on the east side of the creek than on the easier, more level carriage road. The trail is open to horses, but many sections are too rocky and steep for them. Off-road bicycles are permitted, at least for now, but may soon be prohibited on some hillside trails because of an erosion problem and protests from hikers.

Just after crossing the creek, notice a plaque on the left that commemorates baptisms by immersion in the creek by Joseph Gorgas' Seventh Day Baptists in the 1700s. The Gorgas monastery, which stands on the hillside to the right, is now used as a stable. According to legend, its cellars served as a stop on the Underground Railroad. At 5.9 miles cross a deep ravine on Fingerspan, a 59-foot steel footbridge that was built and installed by helicopter in 1987.

At 6.4 miles, you reach the tributary of Cresheim Creek. The bridge is out, but except in periods of high water the creek can be crossed easily on stepping stones. Climbing out of the ravine over several footbridges, you will pass Shakespeare Rock, with a quotation from *The Two Gentlemen of Verona*, and nearby Devils' Pool, said to have limitless depth.

The geology of the gorge is most apparent on the east side of the creek, with its many rock outcroppings. The underlying rock was originally sedimentary, deposited in layers, and then was subjected to intense heat and pressure that caused crystallization into schist, mica, quartzite, and granite. Some of these rocks, such as mica, exhibit layering typical of sedimentary rocks; others, such as granite, are of more uniform composition. Over geologic time these hard rock layers were overlain with layers of silt and sand. The eroding action of the Wissahickon has worn away the softer layers, creating the deep gorge and exposing the harder rocks.

You can readily note the different types of rocks along the creek. The layered rocks, mostly schist, sometimes contain dark red crystals of garnets. Other rocks are smooth and white-gray in color; their surface often has a rippled, flowing appearance, reminding one of their volcanic origin. Be careful: the trail can be slippery after rain, or when leaves cover the smooth rocks.

At 8.0 miles pass under a stone archway, and up a series of steep stone steps. Soon you again have a chance to spot the Indian statue in the trees off to your right, although it may not be easily visible in summer. At 9.0 miles you reach Bells Mill Road. Cross the narrow bridge to return to the parking lot and your car.

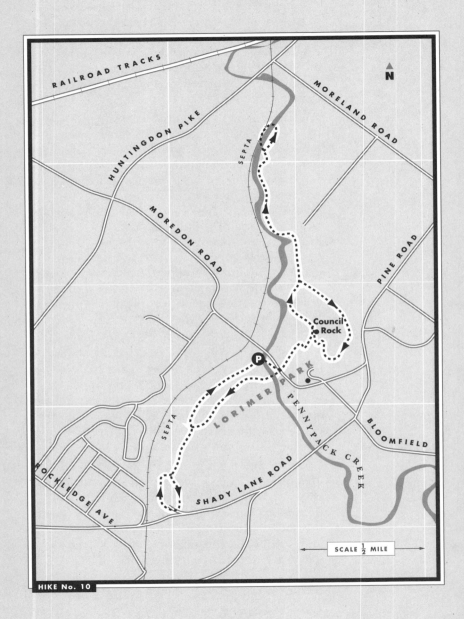

RAILROAD TRACKS

N

HUNTINGDON PIKE

MORELAND ROAD

MOREDON ROAD

SEPTA

PINE ROAD

Council Rock

P

LORIMER PARK

SEPTA

PENNYPACK CREEK

BLOOMFIELD

ROCKLEDGE AVE

SHADY LANE ROAD

SCALE ½ MILE

HIKE No. 10

44

No. 10

Lorimer Park

183 Moredon Road
Huntingdon Valley, PA 19006
(215) 947-3477

Distance	4.6 miles
Elevation	740 feet
Time to hike	2½ hours
Surface	rocky trail; grassy or gravel woods road; trails not blazed or clearly identified
Interesting features	Council Rock, where Indians gathered; abundant berries along old railroad bed
Facilities	water, rest rooms, picnic tables, grills at ranger station
Disability access	no
Hunting	no

Directions **from the Pennsylvania Turnpike (I-276) near Willow Grove:**

1. take exit 27 (Willow Grove), drive south on PA 611 (Easton Road, toward Willow Grove and Jenkintown) 2.1 miles
2. turn left (east) onto PA 63 (Moreland Road)
3. follow PA 63 east (you will make several turns with street name changes) for 3.8 miles
4. turn right (south) on PA 232 (Huntingdon Pike), drive 1.3 miles
5. turn left on Moredon Road, drive 0.9 mile
6. turn right into parking lot for Lorimer Park

Lorimer Park consists of 225 acres located along the Pennypack Creek on the eastern border of Montgomery County with the city of Philadelphia. It is a natural wildlife sanctuary, and more than 70 tree species have been identified in the park. It is also a popular place for ice fishing and sledding in the winter. There are maps available at the visitors' center, but at the time of our last visit they were not accurately drawn.

Walk down the asphalt–gravel road at the north end of the parking lot, under Moredon Road. Continue north along Pennypack Creek, through a mown field toward a ranger station and a flagpole. There is a heavy concentration of (sometimes aggressive) Canada geese in the field and under the pine trees beside the creek. In recent years many geese in the Philadelphia area have become year-round residents near lakes and streams, and are often a nuisance in parks.

Walk through a group of picnic tables to a rustic wooden footbridge. Just over the bridge is a sheer rock face, 40 feet high—Council Rock, where Indians gathered for important meetings. A sign notes that the park was opened October 24, 1938. Turn left to walk upstream along the 80- to 100-foot-wide creek on the Pennypack Trail.

The trail is very rocky at first. At 0.5 mile you will step over a small tributary of the creek and pass a large rock and a trail partially hidden by vegetation on your right. Continue ahead through a floodplain, on one of several crisscrossing trails along the creek. At a large beech tree the trail splits. Bear right, beginning an uphill climb away from the creek.

At 1.3 miles you reach a woods road. Turn left on a road with many large sycamore and oak trees, and begin to go downhill again. At 1.4 miles you will reach another woods road and turn left toward the creek. Turn left again to walk along the edge of the creek. At 2.0 miles you reach the large rock you passed earlier (at 0.5 mile). Turn left on the Boundary Line trail uphill.

Continue straight ahead through several trail intersections. Pass a field on your right at the top of a hill on the park boundary, on a woods road. At the end of the field, pick up the Fireline Trail, then reach another field on your left. Turn right (west) at the end of the field on another woods road.

The trail seems at places to be littered with glass fragments, which on closer inspection turns out to be mica, a shiny mineral of the silicate class. Transparent layers reflect light like tiny mirrors. Turn right again at the next woods road for 500 feet, then left steeply downhill on the Hillside Trail to a wooden covered bridge, which crosses a tributary of the Pennypack. Continue straight ahead to Council Rock and cross the bridge to the picnic area at 2.7 miles.

To explore the southern part of the park, leave the picnic area and cross the field, under Moredon Road, to a gravel road under large yellow-poplars. Cross the small footbridge over the Pennypack and turn left (south) on a woods road (Indian Trail) along Harpers Run. At 3.4 miles the road turns left away from the stream and ascends steadily uphill. At 3.6 miles the road levels and the trees thin out over an open grassy field. The meadow is home to rabbits and mouse-like meadow voles, preyed on by snakes, hawks, and owls. Field wild-flowers attract butterflies in late summer. There is a fence and, beyond that, a cornfield off to the left.

Turn right at another woods road beside a large stone on which is painted "Site of Waterman Mansion—circa 1785." There is no other sign of the old farmstead. Turn right (north) again at a large oak tree. Continue on this woods road through a grove of trees. At 3.8 miles turn left on a grassy road uphill just before completing a loop. At 4.0 miles you will reach the road you walked in on, and you can now begin to backtrack.

Watch for a trail to the left at 4.1 miles. Turn left for 200 feet to an abandoned railroad track. Turn right. The tracks are overgrown with raspberries and blackberries and the terrain drops off steeply on the right. The tracks lead you straight back to the parking lot. All along the last half-mile of the hike you will find plenty of berries (if you are hiking in July or August), which you can conveniently pick just before reaching your car, at 4.6 miles.

Pennypack Wilderness

No. 11

Pennypack Watershed Association
2955 Edge Hill Road
Huntingdon Valley, PA 19006
(215) 657-0830

Distance	3.6 miles
Elevation	280 feet
Time to hike	1¾ hours
Surface	wood-chipped and natural trails, rutted asphalt road
Interesting features	restoration in progress of native habitats of woodlands, marshes, meadows, ponds, and stream; visitors' center with exhibits of interest to children; bird blinds, nesting boxes
Facilities	water, rest rooms at visitors' center; benches along trails; no picnic facilities
Disability access	no
Hunting	no

Directions **from the Pennsylvania Turnpike (I-276) near Willow Grove:**

1. take exit 27 (Willow Grove), drive south on PA 611 (Easton Road, toward Willow Grove and Jenkintown) 0.9 mile

2. turn left onto Fitzwatertown Road (at Dunkin' Donuts)

(continued)

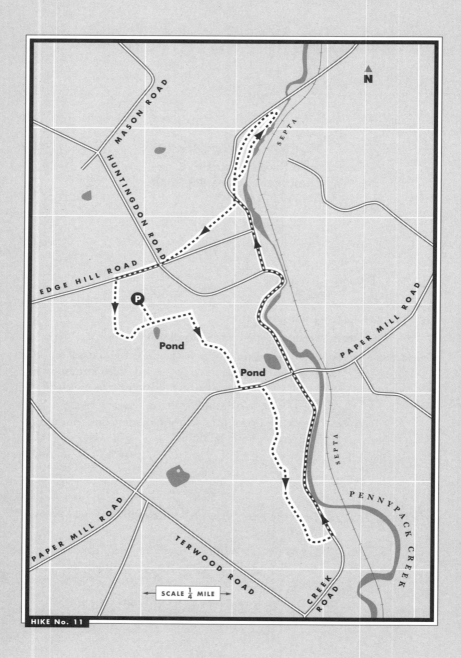

SCALE ¼ MILE

HIKE No. 11

3. cross York Road (PA 263) at 0.6 mile—
   Fitzwatertown Road changes to Terwood Road
   after crossing York
4. continue another 1.7 miles (2.3 miles from PA
   611) to a stop sign
5. turn left on Edge Hill Road, drive 0.4 mile to the
   Pennypack Watershed Association Environmental
   Management Center on the right

Coordinates   40°08'35"N; 75°05'02"W

The Pennypack watershed contains 56 square
miles of land, which drain eventually into the
Delaware River. Of these, more than 400 acres of
forests, wetlands, and meadows are being restored
by the Pennypack Watershed Association, a private,
nonprofit organization dedicated April 24, 1976,
to the restoration of natural habitats in the watershed. Bird walks, bird identification seminars,
and an annual deer census are held. Many animals, including wild turkeys, can be found in the
area. The 10 miles of trails and the visitors' center
are open Monday through Saturday 9:00 a.m. to
5:00 p.m., and Sunday 1:00 to 5:00 p.m.

Begin at the visitors' center, which contains
exhibits, a gift shop, and trail maps, including a
guide to the Wedd Walk, a nature walk. You may
also pick up a map from a wooden box outside
when the center is closed.

Follow the wood-chipped path to the right
of the visitors' center, the Center Trail. There are
flower beds, greenhouses, and solar collector pan-
els along the trail just behind the center. Solar
energy provides 60 percent of the heating needs
for the greenhouses; a wood stove provides auxil-
iary heat.

At a trail intersection, turn left at a labeled
persimmon tree on the Woods Edge Trail; after

another 200 feet you come to another trail inter-section. Here turn right (east) on a path marked "Wetlands Trail" but that according to the associa-tion's map is the Meadow Crossing. Walk east, crossing a meadow with a fence line to the right. At 0.3 mile leave the meadow for woods and another trail intersection. These woods are a 3-acre forest affected by declining trees, deer browsing, and competition from exotic plants. The forest is being restored by the association through plantings of native trees, shrubs, and wildflowers. The Rosebush Trail begins on the left. Continue straight ahead on the Lookout Trail. Plastic tubes 5 feet high encircle and protect several hundred individual saplings along the trail.

At 0.5 mile turn sharply left and downhill (east) along Paper Mill Road, a woods road closed to traffic. Just before reaching a pond on the left with wood ducks, mallards, and Canada geese, turn right up ten steps on the Management Trail. This trail ascends through woods, with a fence to the right and marshy swamplands to the left, and then cuts down a steep embankment, where the trail becomes rocky. You will pass several more sapling nurseries.

You will find various colored blazes on the trees, and not all trail intersections are marked. At 1.3 miles you reach Creek Road, which parallels Pennypack Creek; turn left. Creek Road is a worn, deeply rutted asphalt road closed to traffic. Cross Paper Mill Road and walk past a pond and then wetlands on the left. A fence encircles the area to discourage visitors from approaching too closely and disturbing breeding pairs of shore birds, including herons, grebes, and kingfishers. You will pass a half-dozen private residences along the creek. The Mitchell Trail comes in from the left; this will be your return route. A hundred feet past the trail intersection, turn right on the Wedd Walk.

The Wedd Walk is a nature walk with num-bered signs (the guide is available in the park office) that closely parallels the creek for 0.3 mile. Cross a 50-foot boardwalk over a marshy area, and an old springhouse on the left.

The geology underlying the Pennypack is of interest. Rock formations affect the topography of the area and the formation of soils. The Baltimore formation of gneiss under the Pennypack is very resistant to erosion. As you can see from several points along the creek, it nevertheless has cut its way through cracks in the bedrock to form a narrow floodplain, leaving ridges and exposed rock on either side. The younger, less resistant Stockton rock formation farther north has eroded more, producing finer soils and more rolling terrain.

The Wedd Walk rejoins Creek Road at a stone bridge; turn left on Creek Road and then turn right on the Mitchell Trail at 2.0 miles. After 50 feet the trail turns left, steadily uphill. You pass behind several private residences; at 2.6 miles you will cross paved Huntingdon Road and turn right on the Woods Edge Trail. A split-rail fence is to the right, parallelling Edge Hill Road. You are now on a wood-chipped trail, leading through pine and hemlock trees.

At 3.0 miles cross the entrance road, where the trail becomes Crabapple Meadow Trail. You will see a wildflower meadow to the left. Willow oak (or pin oak), large northern red oak, a grove of hemlock trees, flowering dogwood, and red maple trees are interspersed with open areas and a private residence.

At 3.5 miles you pass a springhouse on the left, and a pond on the right with a fenced dock and bird blind. A pair of Canada geese nests on a small island in the pond; wood ducks also nest here. Black willow, black walnut, and daffodils line the pond. Note the large goldfish and carp in the pond.

Rejoin the Center Trail at this point to return to the visitors' center.

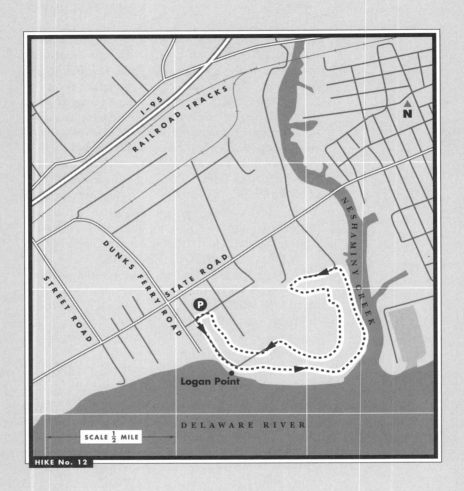

RAILROAD TRACKS

I-95

N

NESHAMINY CREEK

DUNKS FERRY ROAD

STATE ROAD

STREET ROAD

P

Logan Point

DELAWARE RIVER

SCALE ½ MILE

HIKE No. 12

No. 12

Neshaminy Park

Neshaminy State Park

3401 State Road
Bensalem, PA 19020
(215) 639-4538

Distance	3 miles
Elevation	less than 20 feet
Time to hike	1 hour
Surface	woods path, gravel road, asphalt walkway
Interesting features	sea-level estuary under tidal influence; confluence of the Neshaminy Creek with the Delaware River; restoration of tidal marsh
Facilities	water, rest rooms, picnic facilities; swimming pool; Playmasters Theatre Workshop
Disability access	yes, on paved walkways: Logan Walk, East Walk, West Walk; otherwise, no
Hunting	no

Directions **from I-95 near Levittown:**

1. exit at PA 132, drive east on Street Road (SR 2007) 0.6 mile to the T intersection
2. turn left on State Road, drive 0.4 mile
3. park entrance and visitors' center are on your right; park at parking lot on your left

This hike offers a close look at a unique habitat in the Delaware Valley—an estuary. Even though the confluence of the Neshaminy Creek and the Delaware River is 116 miles from the ocean, you are at sea level here. When the tide rises and falls at the ocean in New Jersey, it also rises and falls—an inch a minute—along the river shoreline here. This is called an estuary, and at Neshaminy Creek, the water is fresh, not salt, unlike the water in the lower estuary.

Plants and animals from both salt- and fresh-water habitats live along this section of the river. For example, shad live in the ocean for three to five years, then swim upstream in the spring to spawn in the shallows around Neshaminy. Eels, by contrast, spawn in the Sargasso Sea, in the Caribbean, and migrate to the Delaware in April and May. They live in the river for five to twenty years, returning to the Sargasso Sea to lay eggs and die. Shortnose sturgeon, an endangered species, lives in the estuary but lays eggs upstream.

Native Americans took advantage of the rise and fall of the tides in this area to trap fish. They built fences at the river's edge. At high tide the fish swam over the top of the fence; as the tide went out, the fish were trapped and easily speared.

Begin walking south from the parking lot to Logan Walk, a paved asphalt walkway. Turn right (west). Walk past brick pillars and turn left on Delaware Drive to walk along the Delaware River on a 15-foot-wide asphalt path.

At the bottom of Delaware Drive you will see a large sign for Logan Point. This is a landmark for large ships navigating on the Delaware River. The path narrows to a dirt road and continues as the River Walk.

You will pass several trail intersections; bear right at each one to stay close to the river. Tidal marsh provides habitat to herons, egrets, and sandpipers. One hundred years ago the shoreline here looked very different. Dredging and pollution have destroyed much of the wetlands area along the Delaware. Soil was dredged from the river and used to cover tidal marsh, and a straight channel 24 to 40 feet deep was created to accommodate ore barges. Giant reed and purple loosestrife grow along the banks. Still, the river is slowly improving from its 1970s low point, thanks to environmental regulation. Cattails and wild rice in the shallow waters once again provide food for a large variety of shorebirds.

At 0.3 mile the River Walk narrows to a trail and turns north, leaving the Delaware and following Neshaminy Creek through woodlands. Willows, alders, ashes, and silver maples grow in the moist soil along the creek. In the spring, wild ginger, lesser celandine, and spring beauties bloom. Wood ducks nest in hollow trees near the water. The male has iridescent green, purple, and blue feathers, while the female is grayish in color. Their nests are placed high up in trees to discourage predators such as raccoons and opossums. However, once the chicks hatch in June and join their mothers paddling in the water, snapping turtles take a heavy toll.

At 0.9 mile the trail turns away from the creek, and at 1.0 mile it turns left past brick pillars, onto Logan Walk again. At 1.2 miles, turn left onto a trail through the woods. At 1.3 miles, turn left on a gravel road. At 1.4 miles, bear right at a stand of mature pine trees. Continue straight ahead on the dirt road toward a gate. Notice the grass-covered earthen mounds to your right, called the "soil factory." These mounds were conceived as adding an interesting feature to an otherwise flat landscape, while at the same time providing a place to dispose of treated sludge from the city sewage treatment facility. The project continued until five years ago. Today, the mounds are grass-covered and are mown twice a year. Recently, apple and dogwood trees have been planted nearby. The soil factory is periodically monitored for leaching of any dangerous chemicals.

The flat area to your left is referred to as the "spoils," where silt dredged from the riverbed was dumped. Despite the name and its perhaps unpleasant associations, the soil factory and the spoils are far from barren. Wildflowers, such as red-seeded dandelion and blue toadflax (dainty yellow and orange spikes) thrive. Several types of thistles and milkweed attract butterflies and provide food and cover for many birds. Killdeer nest on the open ground. If you approach the nest, the killdeer will drag a wing and feign injury to lure you away. Bright yellow goldfinches also nest in small shrubs and saplings in the spoils and soil factory.

At 1.7 miles turn right onto an asphalt path. Turn right next at an abandoned parking lot near the river. Continue past a playground and picnic area. At 3.0 miles you return to Logan Walk; the parking lot lies just ahead.

Delhaas Woods and Silver Lake

No. 13

1306 Bath Road
Bristol, PA 19007-2813
(215) 785-1177

Distance	Delhaas Woods, 1.8 miles; Silver Lake, 2.5 miles
Elevation	less than 25 feet
Time to hike	Delhaas Woods, 40 minutes; Silver Lake, 50 minutes
Surface	through Delhaas Woods, woods trail; Silver Lake, boardwalk, woods trail, asphalt walk
Interesting features	Atlantic Coastal Plain geology; woodlands, marsh, meadow, swamp, and bog; bird migration route, especially waterfowl; butterfly garden adjacent to nature center; boardwalks and observation platform overlooking wetlands along Otter Creek; nature center
Facilities	water, rest rooms, picnic tables at the nature center
Disability access	Delhaas Woods, no; Silver Lake, yes
Hunting	no

Directions   **from I-95 near Levittown:**

1. drive south on US 13 (Bristol Pike) for 4.2 miles
2. turn left onto Bath Road (SR 2029) at light
3. continue for 0.8 mile to visitors' center on the right

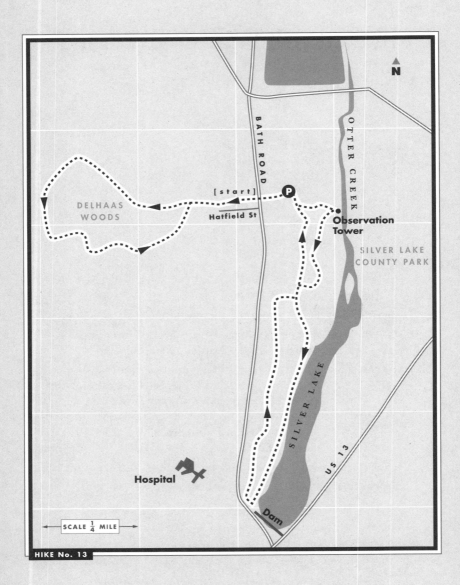

N

BATH ROAD

OTTER CREEK

[start]

P

Hatfield St

Observation
Tower

SILVER LAKE
COUNTY PARK

DELHAAS
WOODS

SILVER LAKE

Hospital

US 13

Dam

SCALE ¼ MILE

HIKE No. 13

Coordinates 40°06'52"N; 74°51'48"W

A narrow strip of land in Pennsylvania running along the Delaware River from Morrisville to Marcus Hook is known geologically as the Atlantic Coastal Plain. The rocks, vegetation, and animals found here differ from those found in the rest of Pennsylvania. The Silver Lake area contains many species more typical of New Jersey or Maryland and found only rarely in Pennsylvania. The red-bellied turtle and southern leopard frog are found in the wetlands. Delhaas Woods is the best remaining example of Atlantic Coastal Plain forest left in Pennsylvania. Much of this area is wetland, which has saved it from development.

Begin this hike by crossing Bath Road to the entrance of Delhaas Woods at the intersection of Bath Road and Hatfield Street. Several boardwalks take you over many small streams and wet areas. Typical trees that thrive in the wet, sandy soil are sweet gum, umbrella magnolia, red maple, and willow oak. Bear right at each of the next two trail intersections, reaching an old railroad grade at 0.6 mile. Turn left and at 0.8 mile, turn left again at a power line cut. Wet meadow is to the left; it had been recently burned when we were there in late summer to clear trees and larger shrubs that were growing under the power line. In spring, the meadow has an abundance of coastal plain wild-flowers, including the Maryland meadow beauty, interspersed with boggy patches of sphagnum moss. The meadow on the right with drier soil conditions supports chickweed, Queen-Anne's lace, goldenrod, thistles, and milkweed.

Continue on the old gravel access road, watching carefully for a trail to the left at 1.0 mile between two power line towers. (If you come to an orange gate, you have walked too far; backtrack, watching carefully for the faint trail.) Cross the meadow to reenter the woods.

At 1.1 miles you will come to an abandoned concrete structure, marked with a faint sign "explosives," behind earthen bunkers. Continue straight ahead. Turn right at the next trail intersection, then continue straight ahead, passing the ruins of two more ammunition storage buildings on the left, located behind 10-foot embankments. These were used to store ammunition during World War II. Complete the loop in Delhaas Woods at 1.4 miles, and retrace your steps to Bath Road.

Cross Bath Road to the parking lot at 1.8 miles. The butterfly garden adjacent to the nature center blooms with flowers in spring, summer, and fall, and attracts a variety of butterflies. The nature center contains exhibits, including live animals (for example, a red-bellied turtle) and fish, as well as a library. The center also organizes bird walks, canoe trips, and ecology programs. It is open Tuesday through Saturday 10:00 a.m. to 5:00 p.m. and Sunday noon to 5:00 p.m.; it is closed Mondays.

On the other side of the center from the butterfly garden, enter the woods at a sign for an outdoor amphitheater. Continue on the woods path, crossing marsh on a long boardwalk. Several steps lead up to a large observation tower overlooking Otter Creek and the upper reaches of the lake. Looking down into the water, you may be surprised—as we were—to see a dozen foot-long catfish looking back at you! Pretty soon several children came along to feed them some bread, and we understood the fish's anticipation.

Continue hiking on woods paths and boardwalks along Silver Lake to observe some of the shyer bird species, such as egrets and herons, and songbirds. Silver Lake is also a refuge for the threatened red-bellied turtle. This turtle (*Chrysemys rubriventris*) grows to an average length of 10 to 12 inches. It is the second-largest turtle in the Philadelphia area (the snapping turtle is the largest).

At 1.0 mile you leave the woods to walk on open lawn and asphalt trails under shade trees. Canada geese, mallard ducks, sea gulls, white-fronted geese, and pigeons congregate here in great numbers at Silver Lake, especially during spring and fall migration. Many people feed the birds, which is not advisable, as such feeding interferes with their migratory patterns. There are picnic tables, playground equipment, and a fitness course along the lake. Continue to walk to the dam. (The trail continues on the eastern side of the lake for another mile, but does not go completely around it.) Follow the asphalt path along Bath Road to return to your car at 2.5 miles.

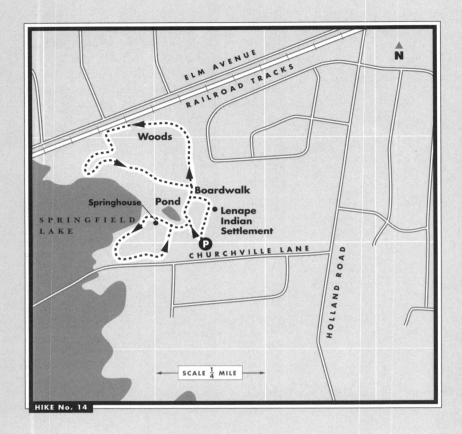

ELM AVENUE

RAILROAD TRACKS

Woods

Boardwalk

Springhouse Pond

SPRINGFIELD
LAKE

Lenape
Indian
Settlement

P

CHURCHVILLE LANE

HOLLAND ROAD

N

SCALE $\frac{1}{4}$ MILE

HIKE No. 14

Churchville Nature Center

No. 14

501 Churchville Lane
Churchville, PA 18966
(215) 357-4005

Distance	1.8 miles
Elevation	less than 25 feet
Time to hike	1 hour
Surface	paved walkways, wood-chipped path, and woods trail
Interesting features	recreated Lenape Indian village, bird observation blind, apiary, wild foods garden, special exhibits for children
Facilities	rest rooms, water at visitors' center; picnic grove; many benches
Disability access	one 0.3-mile wheelchair-accessible trail near visitors' center; otherwise, no
Hunting	no

from US 1 near Levittown:

1. take exit at PA 132, drive west on PA 132 (Street Road), 2.2 miles

2. turn right (north) onto PA 532 (Buck Road), drive 1.8 miles

3. continue straight ahead on Holland Road, drive 0.9 mile, turn left at Churchville Lane

4. drive 0.2 mile on Churchville Lane; Churchville Nature Center is on the right

Coordinates 40°11'12"N; 74°59'31"W

Pick up a map at the visitors' center, which contains interesting touchable exhibits and animals, including honeybees, snakes, turtles, fish, and a tarantula. There is a small library of nature-related books; most volumes can be borrowed. The center offers nature walks, classes, and programs for people of all ages and is open from 10:00 a.m. to 5:00 p.m. everyday except Monday. Trails are open everyday from dawn to dusk. The Dragonfly Niche Gift Shop contains many nature-related articles for sale, including six different varieties of bird seed. Adjacent to the visitors' center are a bird blind, apiary, seed barn, farmhouse, and wildflower garden.

Begin the hike behind the visitors' center by turning right onto the Dragonfly Kroeker Trail. This is a level, paved walkway that leads to a pond and back for a 0.3-mile circle route for the wheeled hiker. The other trails are not paved but are fairly level and well maintained, and they could be managed by the wheelchair hiker in good condition.

The trail as described generally follows the perimeter of the park, first through an overgrown meadow and then woods. At 0.1 mile there is a short trail leading to a recreated Lenape Indian settlement. Continue on the asphalt trail; at 0.2 mile turn right to follow the green arrows of the Leafdown Trail. This leads across a marsh on a boardwalk. You will find many flowers here, especially in spring: notably Jack-in-the-pulpit, violets, and marsh ferns.

As you enter the woods, notice the diversity of tree varieties, including hazelnut, beech, black tupelo (sour gum), dogwood, sassafras, as well as maple and oak. In open meadows black and red raspberries are plentiful and make for a nice snack in July. The Leafdown Trail follows the perimeter of the park through woods and meadows to Springfield Lake (Churchville Reservoir) at 1.0 mile.

At 1.4 miles you reach the edge of a quiet pond and then an old (mid-1800s) springhouse. At the springhouse go straight ahead, following orange arrows to the edge of the lake again at 1.5 miles. At the lake, look for an eagle or osprey nest on a platform over the water. Turn left, following the trail along the lake. Except in winter you will probably see ducks or other waterfowl along the edge. Continue following the orange arrows to a pine plantation on the right. The trail leads back to the springhouse and the pond, and returns from there to the visitors' center.

You will find that it is easy to figure out additional routes through the nature center grounds, using the well-drawn park map.

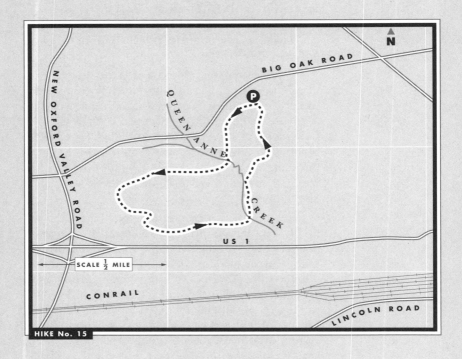

N

NEW OXFORD VALLEY ROAD

BIG OAK ROAD

QUEEN ANNE

CREEK

P

US 1

SCALE ½ MILE

CONRAIL

LINCOLN ROAD

HIKE No. 15

68

No. 15

Five-Mile Woods Preserve

Five-Mile Woods Nature Preserve
1305 Big Oak Road
Yardley, PA 19067
(215) 493-6652

Distance	2.8 miles
Elevation	85 feet
Time to hike	1¼ hours
Surface	woods trail, boardwalk
Interesting features	located on the Fall Line, the boundary between the Atlantic Coastal Plain and the Piedmont Plateau geologic regions; remnants of bog habitat
Facilities	rest rooms, water at visitors' center
Disability access	no
Hunting	no

Directions **from US 1 near Levittown:**

1. drive north on New Oxford Valley Road for 0.4 mile
2. turn right onto Big Oak Road, drive 1.1 miles
3. turn right into Five-Mile Woods

Coordinates 40°12'12"N; 74°51'02"W

The low-lying Five-Mile Woods Preserve is a 285-acre forest and one of the few natural sections of the fall line remaining in Pennsylvania. The fall line refers to the boundary between the Coastal Plain and the Piedmont Plateau. The preserve contains the distinctive sandy soils and vegetation of areas farther east in New Jersey, as well as the deciduous forests typical farther west. This preserve also contains the only remaining cranberry bog in Bucks County. Several rare-to-Pennsylvania and endangered species of plants and animals may be found here.

The preserve contains miles of crisscrossing trails, and a well-drawn and accurate map is available in a box at the courtyard of the headquarters building, just beyond the parking lot. The route described generally follows the perimeter of the park. If you wish to take a shorter hike, you can follow one of several cutback routes to return to your car.

From the courtyard, proceed south and then bear right on the wood-chipped Sphagnum Trail. A wooden boardwalk passes over areas of bog. Bog is defined as wetland with very limited exchange of water. Lacking aeration, a bog becomes acidic; nutrients such as nitrogen, calcium, and phosphorus are locked up in the vegetation instead of being recycled. A very specialized plant community develops in response to the acidity and lack of nutrients. The dominant plant is sphagnum moss. The sphagnum produces tannic acid, making the water even more acidic and hostile to many other plants. Those that can survive the wet acidic environment include honeysuckle (or swamp azalea), six species of native orchids, including the small whorled pogonia and the pink lady's slipper, and cranberry, which produces berries in the fall. Five-Mile Woods may also be the only remaining habitat in Pennsylvania of the New Jersey chorus frog.

Bear right on the Five-Mile Trail. Here you will find beeches, maples, and other hardwoods interspersed with swampy areas crossed by boardwalks. At 0.5 mile, turn right, crossing Queen Anne Creek. Soon you reach the Evergreen Trail; turn right. This leads to an overgrown pine plantation, followed by large hemlock trees.

At 1.0 mile turn right at an intersection with the Ridge Trail. This trail shortly turns sharply left and downhill to the Coastal Plain Trail. The Atlantic Coastal Plain refers to the area east of here in New Jersey. Soils are sandy, poorly drained, and low in nutrients. Dry areas support scrubby pine, oak, laurel, and huckleberry. Continue to the Five-Mile Trail again, turn right at 1.5 miles, and cross Queen Anne Creek again at 2.0 miles at the Piedmont Trail.

Vegetation here is more typical of the terrain farther west, where richer soils support a variety of oaks and beeches. Bear right on the Heath Trail, leaving the creek. Then bear right on the Sweetgum Trail to an open classroom, dominated by a large sweetgum tree, just before returning to the visitors' center at 2.8 miles.

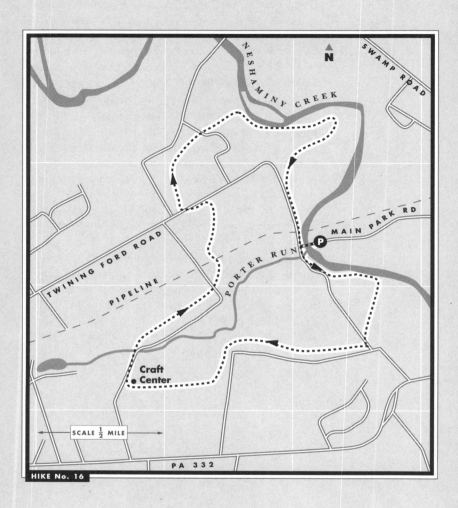

N

NESHAMINY CREEK

SWAMP ROAD

MAIN PARK RD

P

PORTER RUN

TWINING FORD ROAD

PIPELINE

Craft
Center

SCALE ½ MILE

PA 332

HIKE No. 16

Tyler State Park

No. 16

101 Swamp Road
Newtown, PA 18940
(215) 968-2021

Distance	5.1 miles
Elevation	400 feet
Time to hike	2¼ hours
Surface	paved asphalt path, in good condition
Interesting features	a 5- to 8-foot-wide paved trail through Pennsylvania farmlands and forests; original stone farm dwellings dating back to the early 1700s
Facilities	water, rest rooms (wheelchair-accessible rest room at the parking lot), grills, and picnic tables at the trailhead; water and picnic tables at two other locations on the trail
Disability access	yes
Hunting	no

Directions **from US 1 near Levittown:**

1. drive north on PA 413 for 5.5 miles
2. turn left onto Swamp Road entry (park entrance) at traffic light
3. drive 0.3 mile through park (pass park office at 0.2 mile)
4. turn right at 0.3 mile onto Main Park Road
5. continue another 1.2 miles to parking lot on the right

The outstanding feature of Tyler State Park is its potential for enjoyment by anyone, regardless of age or level of athletic ability. It is as accessible to young children, older adults, strollers, and wheelchair hikers as it is to the hiker on foot. The hike as described is 5.1 miles, but there are 10.5 miles of paved trails, 4 miles of gravel hiking trails, and 9 miles of bridle trails throughout the 1,711 acres of the park. The trails wind through scenic woodlands, along Neshaminy Creek, and adjacent to fields under cultivation. They afford a close-up and educational view of agriculture in Bucks County. When walking the trails, stay to the right. Bicyclists and joggers pass on your left. The park is not overused, even on a lovely late-summer Saturday. There is no hunting at any time, so it can be enjoyed all year.

A good first stop is at the visitors' center, where you can pick up a well-drawn and accurate map. There are many ways to shorten (or lengthen) the hike described here.

Park at the parking lot and turn right downhill toward Neshaminy Creek. (There is wheelchair-accessible parking for one vehicle farther down, right next to the creek.) Cross the creek on a concrete pedestrian bridge. Several families of ducks and geese nest here; visitors are requested not to feed them, so as to not interfere with their migratory habits. The creek is about 100 feet wide. There is a 3-foot-high dam a short distance upstream, which slows and widens the creek to 150 feet and accommodates a canoe launch area. This area freezes in winter and is used for ice skating.

After crossing the creek, you reach a T intersection at the Mill Dairy Trail. Turn left uphill through mixed hardwoods, with Neshaminy Creek to your left. At 0.3 mile bear left on the Woodfield Trail. You pass a number of exercise stations on your right. These were quite popular a few years ago but now are in some disrepair.

At 0.5 mile the trees thin out somewhat as you turn away from the creek. The trail is lined on both sides with black walnut trees. In late summer they are a favorite for tentworms. The trees are not usually damaged by infestation, but the nests are unsightly.

At 0.6 mile at a T intersection, turn left across a wooden bridge on the Mill Dairy Trail. Walk 50 feet and then turn right on the Stable Mill Trail. At 1.5 miles the Natural Area Trail comes in from the right at a cornfield. Make a 90-degree left turn, staying on the Stable Mill Trail. There is a thin line of small trees and shrubs on both sides of the trail, beyond which lie agricultural fields of corn and soybeans. One-quarter of the park is under cultivation. Crops typically grown include winter wheat, corn, soybeans, hay, and milo, with tall plumes, which is used for birdseed. The agricultural ground leases are awarded to the highest bidder, which supports the park operation. Farming has been a tradition on this land for more than 300 years, and the changing agricultural crops provide frequent changes of scenery.

At 1.7 miles you will reach the Pennsylvania Guild of Craftsmen Craft Center on the right, opposite a parking lot; here you can buy various locally made arts and craft items. Continue straight ahead to a stop sign, then turn right on the Number 1 Lane Trail. The trail immediately crosses Porter Run, a small feeder stream, on a wooden bridge. There is a bird blind in front of a bird feeding station along the stream.

The trail is quite level here through a park-like setting with picnic tables under large maples, oaks, and pines. Alongside the trail are several old Pennsylvania farmhouses, many dating from the early 1700s. These historic farm dwellings are currently being lived in and maintained privately by persons who lease the state-owned homes.

At 2.5 miles cross another tributary of Porter Run on a stone bridge. From here the trail heads uphill into woodlands again. In a few minutes you will leave the woods and find yourself again walking through cornfields, with large ash and European beech trees between the trail and the fields. Pass another farmhouse, and a water fountain and picnic table.

At 3.0 miles reach a T intersection with the Dairy Hill Trail, which has been very recently paved (all the trails are well-maintained, semi-smooth asphalt for good traction). Turn left steeply uphill. Cornfields lie on both sides. At 3.1 miles turn right on the White Pine Trail, then pass a stable on the left. Horses can be boarded here and also leased for riding on the bridle trails in the park.

After a moderate uphill climb, you will reach an intersection with the Covered Bridge Trail. (A left turn on this trail leads 0.2 mile to Neshaminy Creek and the Schofield Ford Covered Bridge. The bridge, burned in 1991, is now under restoration.) This spot at the top of a hill affords a lovely view to the north across rolling countryside and farms, a water fountain, and picnic table. Continue straight ahead, leaving the White Pine Trail for the Dairy Hill Trail.

This trail leads downhill through mixed hardwoods, and at 3.7 miles you reach Neshaminy Creek, down a steep embankment. Walk parallel to the creek, turning away from it at 4.0 miles. At 4.8 miles, turn left at an intersection with the Mill Dairy Trail and then cross a stone bridge. At 4.9 miles, pass the historic Thompson Dairy House. It is not open to the public, but note the cornerstone reading 1775. The Mill Dairy Trail leads back to the creek and the pedestrian bridge. Cross Neshaminy Creek to return to the parking lot and your car at 5.1 miles.

Audubon Wildlife Sanctuary

No. 17

Audubon and Pawlings Roads
Audubon, PA 19407
(610) 666-5593

Distance	Green Trail, 1.0 mile loop; can be extended to 2.0 miles by adding other trails
Elevation	90 feet
Time to hike	½ hour
Surface	some steep trails through woods and meadows; many crisscrossing trails not always well marked, but impossible to get lost (just 130 acres)
Interesting features	site of Mill Grove, the first home in America of John James Audubon, artist and naturalist; 170 acres of steep slopes, open meadows, and mowed lawns on the east bank of Perkiomen Creek; exhibits of many of Audubon's paintings and drawings, including an original edition of *The Birds of America*, consisting of four large volumes of engraved life-sized prints, the cornerstone of Audubon's work
Disability access	to mansion and museum only; trails not accessible
Facilities	water, rest rooms at visitors' center; benches along trail; no picnicking allowed (ask for directions at the visitors' center to Lower Perkiomen Park, where there is picnicking with a view of Mill Grove)
Hunting	no

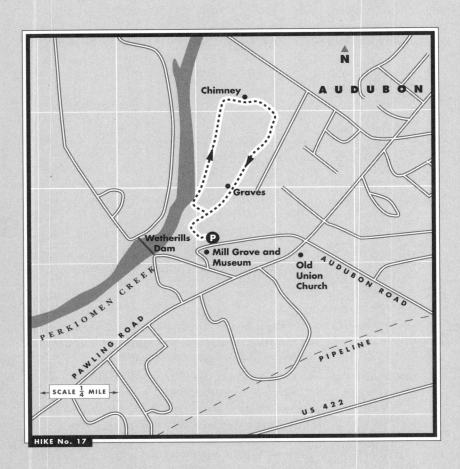

Chimney

A U D U B O N

N

Graves

Wetherills
Dam

P

Mill Grove and
Museum

Old
Union
Church

A U D U B O N   R O A D

P E R K I O M E N   C R E E K

PAWLING ROAD

PIPELINE

U S   4 2 2

←| SCALE ¼ MILE |→

HIKE No. 17

from US 202 near King of Prussia:

1. drive west on US 422 for 2.2 miles (toward Pottstown–Reading)

2. exit at PA 363 north (turn right at stop sign), drive 0.2 mile (if you are driving east on PA 422, you cannot exit on PA 363; you will need to turn around and approach PA 363 westbound on 422)

3. turn left at first light onto Audubon Road

4. drive 1.2 miles; the road deadends at Mill Grove on Pawling Road; follow signs to the parking lot

Coordinates   40°07'25"N; 75°25'34"W

Mill Grove was built in 1762 and was purchased in 1789 by Lieutenant Commander Jean Audubon, a French sea captain, for investment purposes. In 1804 Captain Audubon sent his eighteen-year-old son, John James, to supervise the estate, which included a working lead mine.

Young Audubon lived at Mill Grove only a short time, a little more than two years, but spent much of this time exploring the wooded hills along Perkiomen Creek and the Schuylkill River. Here he observed, collected, and sketched the native wildlife, especially birds. Audubon became fascinated with the depiction of birds in natural settings and poses, a new concept for his day. Here at Mill Grove he courted and married Lucy Bakewell; they moved to Kentucky, and then later to New York. The mine, unsuccessful under the young overseer, was sold in 1806 to Francis DaCosta, who had been young Audubon's partner. It later did achieve financial success under the Wetherill family; the mining of lead ore supported the family paint business.

From the parking lot, which is surrounded by apple trees, walk past the Education Center and barn on your left and continue to the Audubon

Mansion and Museum. No admission fee is charged for entrance to the museum and trails. The grounds are open from Tuesday to Sunday 7:00 a.m. to dusk. The museum is open 10:00 a.m. until 4:00 p.m. Tuesday through Saturday and 1:00 to 4:00 p.m. on Sundays. It is closed on Mondays, Christmas Day, New Year's Day, and Thanksgiving Day. The mansion is surrounded by bird feeders, baths, and nesting boxes to attract the birds as well as benches to rest and enjoy them. One hundred and eighty-one species have been sighted at Mill Grove since 1953; sixty species of birds have been found nesting within the preserve.

Follow the signs to the Green Trail, marked with yellow diamonds and green blazes on some trees. On the way, you pass the site of the old lead mine on the property. At 0.2 mile you come to a trail intersection and twin stone bridges. Bear left just after the bridges and walk uphill through a hemlock forest. At the top of the hill you have a wonderful view overlooking Perkiomen Creek and the lower Perkiomen Valley Park on the other side. Turning away from the creek, walk up a steep wooded slope, on 20 wooden steps. There are several intersecting trails here; just keep to the left, paralleling the creek. Turn right at an old brick chimney that was used for the smelting of copper ore. Behind the chimney is the abandoned copper mine shaft and mine dumps. Covered by rotting boards and earth, the mine shaft off the trail is not safe for exploring.

After a few hundred feet the trail turns sharply right (west). Continue past a small fenced grave-yard of miners on the right. Only one unreadable partial headstone is visible under a large hackberry tree. Walk along the edge of a meadow and down a short hill, where the Green Trail rejoins the twin bridges. Retrace your steps to the museum.

Audubon Wildlife Sanctuary

Audubon's home is a restored fieldstone farm-house, the only home lived in by Audubon still standing in America. It is where Audubon began his, as he called it, "simple and agreeable studies" of birds. Exhibits explain how he developed his technique of shooting them and immediately mounting them on a wire armature to hold them in lifelike positions to draw. Audubon was the first to study their habits and migration by an early form of banding, tying silver threads around the legs of Eastern phoebes. Nearly every room of his home contains his paintings. There are also works by other artists, including "Birds in Porcelain" by Edward Marshall Boehm, a mineral collection, copperplate engravings, period antiques, and stuffed birds and mammals. Mill Grove now displays all of the major works published by the famous artist, naturalist, and author.

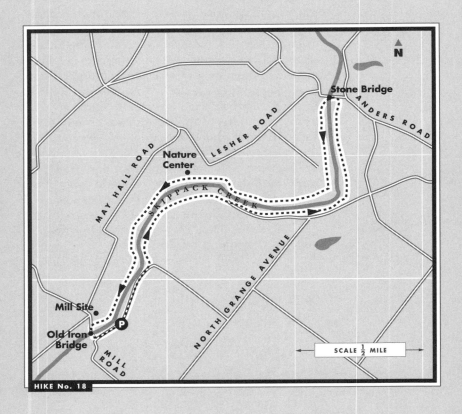

N

Stone Bridge

ANDERS ROAD

LESHER ROAD

MAY HALL ROAD

Nature
Center

SKIPPACK CREEK

NORTH GRANGE AVENUE

Mill Site

Old Iron
Bridge

P

MILL ROAD

SCALE ½ MILE

HIKE No. 18

No. 18

Skippack Creek

Evansburg State Park
May Hall Road
Collegeville, PA 19426
(215) 409-1150

Distance	5 miles
Elevation	225 feet
Time to hike	2½ hours
Surface	rocky trail
Interesting features	Skippack Creek; more than fifty pre-Revolutionary dwellings; the visitors' center, built in the early 1700s, contains exhibits on early German Mennonite life and the natural history of the area; remnants of an old grist mill
Facilities	rest rooms, water, picnic tables near Nature Center (at 4 miles)
Disability access	no
Hunting	yes

Directions **from US 202 near King of Prussia:**

1. drive west on PA 422 for 8.2 miles (toward Pottstown) to PA 29

2. turn right (north toward Collegeville) onto PA 29, drive 2.4 miles

(continued)

3. bear right on Ridge Pike, drive 0.2 mile, crossing Perkiomen Creek bridge
4. turn left onto Germantown Pike, drive 2.0 miles
5. turn left onto North Grange Avenue, drive 0.7 mile
6. turn left onto Mill Road, drive 0.7 mile, park in the lot on the right side

Coordinates 40°11'26"N; 75°24'20"W

The Skippack Creek trail is a 5-mile loop marked with white diamond blazes; it runs along both sides of Skippack Creek and past many points of historic interest. Begin by crossing Mill Road and turning right to walk upstream on the trail running along the edge of Skippack Creek. At 0.2 mile, after walking a short stretch on the road, you turn left, away from it to continue along the creek. In early spring we saw several pairs of mallard ducks and a large heron fishing in the creek.

At 0.4 mile the trail turns right, away from the creek. At 0.5 mile you will cross a horse trail. Continue ahead on the sometimes muddy trail, with planks across the wetter areas. Walk through a stand of large beech trees, notable for the smooth light-gray bark, especially noticeable when the leaves are off the trees. At 0.8 mile you will cross the horse trail again and continue straight ahead toward the stream. The trail becomes steeper as you walk halfway up a ridge line, with the creek 100 feet below (the elevation here is 150 feet). The trees are mixed hardwoods and hemlocks.

The trail levels off, then crosses a deep (20 foot) gully on a bridge at 1.3 miles. The trail gradually descends to the level of Skippack Creek. You may hear woodpeckers; look for animal tracks along the shallow banks of the stream. Some of the common wildlife to be found here are blue jays, flickers, white-breasted nuthatches, and gray and red squirrels. At 2.0 miles turn left on Anders Road (closed to traffic) to cross an old stone bridge over the creek. After crossing, make a sharp left turn on a dirt trail marked with a hiking symbol and walk to the top of a rise.

At 2.3 miles you will pass under a high-tension line at a power line cut. Here you will see many briars, small shrubs, and cedar trees. At 2.5 miles you will pass an old white stone house and spring-house, built by Isaac Cassel in 1771. This German farmhouse is known as the Lesher Farm. At 2.8 miles you will cross a small feeder stream on a wooden footbridge. At 3.1 miles notice the farm fields on the right. The trail splits; bear right, following the hiker symbols and the white diamonds. At 3.3 miles the trail turns right away from the stream to follow the edge of a cornfield.

Pass another old farmhouse dating from 1854, the End house. This area is at low elevation, with walkways built over the muddy places. In spring you may find an abundance of wildflowers: pink lady's slippers, violets, Jack-in-the-pulpits, and trillium.

At 3.6 miles you come to an intersection with the Old Farmstead Trail, which turns right. Continue straight ahead on the Skippack Creek Trail. Several signs along this section of the trail describe the natural history and geology of the area.

Skippack Creek draws its name from the Lenape Indian word *skippau-hacki*, meaning "wetland." The Skippack's water supplied the power for the operation of many colonial mills. The pitch of Skippack Creek was ideal for water wheels. Seven mills once operated here: five grist mills, a saw and grist mill, and a fulling mill, for the processing of wool into felt.

Sandstone forms the channel of the stream. From 1860 to 1915 this sandstone, also called brownstone, was quarried for building material for homes, barns, and fences. Pennsylvania brownstone was also exported for building projects from Florida to New York and as far west as St. Louis.

The trail ascends rather steeply (to 200 feet) at 4.0 miles. The terrain drops off abruptly on the left side to the Skippack 150 feet below. The Nature Center, in a building that was built in 1734, is on the right; also available here are picnic tables, grills, rest rooms, and water.

From 4.5 to 4.8 miles the trail follows a mill race built 240 years ago. The Markley Mill, a saw and grist mill, was operated here by Henry Pennypacker's sons from 1752 to 1795. Finely built arches and the dam site are still visible. The miller's house dating from 1753 is also along the trail.

At 4.8 miles you will cross the creek again on an old iron bridge. Turn left to walk between the stream and Mill Road, returning to the parking lot and your car at 5.0 miles.

No 19

Betzville Railroad Grade–Schuylkill River Trail

Valley Forge National Historical Park

Route 23 and North Gulph Road
Valley Forge, PA 19481
(610) 783-1077

Distance	6.2 miles
Elevation	50 feet
Time to hike	2½ hours
Surface	grassy railroad grade, woods road and trail
Interesting features	Schuylkill River; railroad grade; historic interest—supply route for General Washington's encampment at Valley Forge
Facilities	water, rest rooms, picnic tables, grills at start of hike (at Betzville parking lot); benches along Schuylkill River Trail
Disability access	Schuylkill River Trail is fully acccessible; otherwise, no
Hunting	no

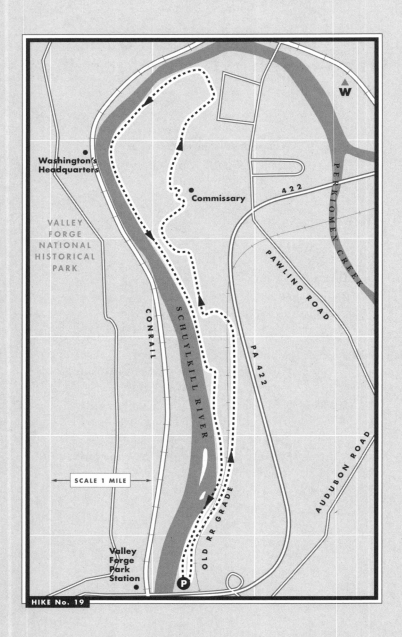

Washington's
Headquarters

Commissary

VALLEY
FORGE
NATIONAL
HISTORICAL
PARK

W

4 2 2

PERKIOMEN CREEK

PAWLING ROAD

PA 422

CONRAIL

SCHUYLKILL RIVER

AUDUBON ROAD

SCALE 1 MILE

OLD R R GRADE

Valley
Forge
Park
Station

P

from US 202 near King of Prussia:

1. drive west on US 422 for 2.2 miles

2. exit onto PA 363 south (turn left at stop sign) (if you are driving east on US 422 you cannot exit on PA 363; you will need to turn around and approach PA 363 westbound on 422)

3. drive 0.3 mile, turn left onto Betzwood Lane, then right, at the Betzwood picnic area; park in the parking lot on the right

Coordinates 40°06'35"N; 75°25'17"W

Although part of Valley Forge National Historical Park, this hike is across the Schuylkill River from the major encampments and historic points of interest in the park. As a result, it is much less used. As you leave the parking lot, turn east on a wide asphalt path on the bike route. Turn left at a T intersection at 0.1 mile, along an old grassy rail-road grade. Tracks and ties have been removed from the abandoned Pennsylvania Railroad grade. (The paved bike trail turns right to go under the Betzwood bridge and can be followed all the way into Philadelphia to the Art Museum via the Manayunk Canal towpath.)

At 0.6 mile you cross a power line cut; continue straight ahead. At 1.2 miles walk around a gate, fairly close to the highway. After walking 500 feet, you will reach the edge of a farmer's field. Turn left, leaving the abandoned railroad grade to follow the park boundary on a woods road that is closed to traffic.

At 1.8 miles you will reach the power line cut again. (If you continue straight ahead for 500 feet, you will reach the Schuylkill River Trail. A left turn here will take you 1 mile back to the parking lot, and 0.5 mile farther to your car, for a total hiking distance of 3.3 miles.)

For a longer hike of 6.2 miles, turn right at the power line cut, following the hiker symbol on a metal pole. You are now on a narrow, graveled road, heading west under the power line. At 1.9 miles, the trail leaves the power line on a grassy road through second-growth woods. Continue straight ahead along a farmer's field, on the park boundary. At 2.1 miles, veer left away from the field, following the dirt road into the woods. The road narrows to a trail and crosses a small stream on a wooden footbridge.

At 2.4 miles you will leave the woods at the edge of a grassy meadow. Notice the large stone barn and several stone outbuildings across the field. This is the site of the commissary for General George Washington's troops. Blacksmiths, wheelwrights, leather workers, and other skilled laborers worked here on the wagons, muskets, cartridge boxes, and other equipment necessary to support the encampment.

Continue northwest across the field on a path, turn left on a gravel road to walk west and then walk around a gate at 2.5 miles in second-growth woods. The woods road is smooth and level, closed to traffic. At 3.0 miles turn left on a trail that follows along a gas pipeline, just before a house. At 3.2 miles turn left onto the Schuylkill River Trail.

The Schuylkill River Trail is a wide, smooth path with many benches along the way, suitable for bicycles, strollers, or wheelchair hikers. Large sycamore, walnut, and oak trees line the trail. The river, only 20 feet away on your right, is very wide at this point; Valley Creek joins the Schuylkill just adjacent to the Valley Forge railroad station on the other side of the river. There is evidence of recent flooding along the trail. Well-maintained footbridges cross several tributaries. Along here, we were able to approach a group of five deer to within 50 feet, and we also spotted a young raccoon on the trail.

The Schuylkill River was the American army's northern defense and a major supply route for General Washington's army during the winter of 1777–1778. Food supplies were ferried down the river from Pennsylvania farms. White clay taken from the banks of the river was used as mortar for the soldiers' wooden huts. In early June, because of sanitation problems and disease in the huts, General Washington ordered his troops into tents on this side of the river. Nearby is the Fatland ford, where equipment and troops were ferried across the river. At 4.9 miles you reach a large rock, marked as the site of General Sullivan's bridge, built in 1777–1778 to facilitate military operations and to allow for a quick evacuation of Valley Forge in case of a British siege. According to the inscription on the rock, the bridge was "destroyed by freshets in the winter of 1778–9."

At 5.7 miles you will reach the northern end of the Betzwood parking lot. This is a popular, level area for in-line skating (rollerblading). Continue past picnic tables, grills, rest rooms, and water to your car at 6.2 miles.

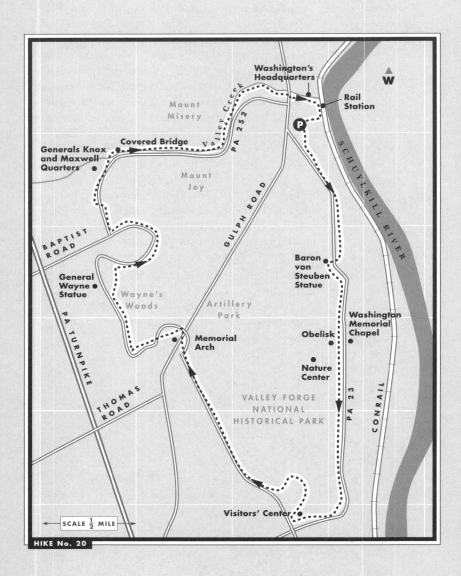

W

Washington's
Headquarters

Rail
Station

Mount
Misery

Covered Bridge

Generals Knox
and Maxwell
Quarters

PA 252

Valley Creek

SCHUYLKILL RIVER

Mount
Joy

GULPH ROAD

BAPTIST
ROAD

General
Wayne
Statue

Wayne's
Woods

Artillery
Park

Baron
von
Steuben
Statue

PA TURNPIKE

Memorial
Arch

Obelisk

Washington
Memorial
Chapel

Nature
Center

THOMAS
ROAD

VALLEY FORGE
NATIONAL
HISTORICAL PARK

PA 23

CONRAIL

Visitors' Center

SCALE ½ MILE

Valley Forge

No. 20

Valley Forge National Historical Park
Route 23 and North Gulph Road
Valley Forge, PA 19481
(610) 783-1077

Distance	6.8 miles
Elevation	325 feet
Time to hike	2¾ hours
Surface	multi-use paved trail; dirt and gravel path
Interesting features	site of Revolutionary War winter encampment of General Washington's troops in 1777–1778
Facilities	water, rest rooms at several locations; picnicking in designated areas
Disability access	yes, except for 0.1 mile along Valley Creek Road
Hunting	no

Directions **from US 202 near King of Prussia:**

1. drive west on US 422 for 1.6 miles

2. turn left (west) onto PA 23 (Valley Forge), go through two traffic lights, then bear right at 0.2 mile (following PA 23); the Valley Forge visitors' center is on the left

3. continue past the visitors' center on PA 23, drive 2.4 miles, then turn right into parking lot at Washington's Headquarters

Valley Forge is a great place for walking, bicycling, cross-country skiing, sledding, and kite flying. It is best known, of course, for the history that surrounds the visitor to the park. Accurate reconstructions make the winter of 1777–1778 seem to come alive. One can imagine von Steuben drilling the troops on the Grand Parade, the difficult existence of the ordinary soldier living in damp and crowded huts, and the heroic figure of General Washington on horseback surveying the troops.

Begin walking at the edge of the parking lot at Washington's Headquarters, turning left, back toward the visitors' center. You are walking on a paved multi-use trail with a yellow dividing line. Signs advise walking on the right, especially at busy times; the left side is used for passing bicycles.

The terrain is open and rolling, with fine views of the countryside. After passing several monuments and soldiers' huts, you reach a picnic area at 0.7 mile. The path then crosses PA 23 to a statue of Baron Friedrich von Steuben gazing across the vast grass-covered Grand Parade. Von Steuben, a Prussian volunteer, drilled the regiments into an effective fighting force.

As you continue along this trail, you will pass General James Mitchell Varnum's quarters on the right and, at 1.2 miles, the Washington Memorial Chapel and the Valley Forge Historical Museum on the left. These are privately owned but open daily (admission fees of $1.50 for adults and $0.50 for children under 16 are charged for the museum). On the right, a stone path leads to Waterman's monument, a 50-foot stone obelisk at the only identified grave at Valley Forge.

Just past the obelisk a road leads 0.1 mile to the site of Jedediah Huntington's quarters, which has been used as a nature center since 1995. Featuring hands-on exhibits, it is open Tuesdays, Thursdays, and Saturdays from noon to 4 p.m. At 2.3 miles you pass the visitors' center on the right. An audio-visual program and displays explain the history of the encampment; no fee is charged.

Continuing on the path, you walk along a ridge following the "outer line defenses." Earthworks on the left side were built to protect the encampments on the right. At 2.6 miles, you reach the site of the first encampment, that of Brigadier General John Peter Muhlenberg's brigade, consisting of a group of eight reconstructed log huts. Twelve soldiers lived in each log hut, which was 14 by 16 feet and only 6½ feet high. The huts were built along a street that parallels the path you are following. On summer weekends, interpreters in period costumes demonstrate the conditions of the Revolutionary soldier's life.

Continuing, you pass monuments of five additional brigades on Outer Line Drive. At 3.3 miles you will pass the National Memorial Arch on a hill. The arch was built in 1917 and commemorates the "patience and fidelity" of the 18,000 soldiers who wintered at Valley Forge. As many as 2,000 men, weakened by inadequate food and poor conditions, died of typhoid, dysentery, pneumonia, and other diseases during the terrible winter of 1777–1778.

To the right, one-half mile away on a facing ridge, you can see the cannons of Artillery Park. Here artillery was stored and repaired, and gun crews were drilled and trained. It was in a central location for quick deployment and readiness for a British attack that never came.

At 3.9 miles you reach a picnic area and the edge of Wayne's Woods. Follow the path along the edge of the woods. To the left, marked by a small flag and plaque, lies the grave of an unknown Revolutionary soldier.

At 4.7 miles the multi-use trail splits at the base of Mount Joy. A turn to the right will lead you 1.0 mile back to von Steuben's statue, past more soldiers' huts; this is a completely accessible route for wheelchairs, strollers, and bicycles. As described below, the hike includes 0.1 mile along Valley Creek Road; this section cannot be recommended for a wheeled hiker, as the road is narrow.

Continue straight ahead on the multi-use trail through a section of mixed hardwoods. Soon you enter an open field again. Across Valley Creek Road is an airfield for model planes, in fairly continuous use in good weather. Cross to a parking lot at 5 miles. The multi-use trail ends here at the parking lot; you will continue on an narrow asphalt road, passing several Revolutionary-era farmhouses. These are the quarters used by General Henry Knox and General William Maxwell, and are not open to the public. Turn right and walk past the stables and grazing horses to return to Valley Creek Road. From here you turn left and walk along the road for 0.1 mile to a covered bridge, built in 1865. The bridge is still in use today.

You will cross Valley Creek over the covered bridge at 5.3 miles; look for the wide footpath to your right. Walk downstream along the creek through shady and pleasant woods. The steep and rock-covered slope of Mount Misery is to your left; Mount Joy is to your right across Valley Creek Road. At 6.3 miles you will reach the site of the upper forge. Valley Forge was named for the two iron forges built along the creek in the 1740s. By the time of the Revolution, a sawmill and gristmill had been added. You can see the remains of a low stone dam used to power the bellows and hammer. During the winter encampment, a road was cut through the hill directly in front of you and was used to take materials to the troops from the forge and mills.

Continue on the path downstream. You are likely to see ducks and abundant fish in the creek, and deer on the hillsides. At 6.4 miles turn to the left (west) away from the stream. At 6.6 miles you will reach an intersection with the yellow-blazed Horseshoe Trail; turn right. The trail, a narrow gravel road, passes several dwellings that served as shops and quarters for skilled artisans such as blacksmiths, wheelwrights, and leather workers. The trail leads back to the stream and PA 23. Turn right, crossing Valley Creek on an old stone bridge. On the other side a large stone marks the start of the Horseshoe Trail, a 130-mile-long rugged trail from here to Stony Mountain in Dauphin County.

Cross PA 23 and walk toward the traffic light for 100 feet. Turn left on a dirt and gravel road toward Washington's Headquarters. The buildings are open 9 a.m.–5 p.m. (There is a fee of $2.00 for adults to tour the Headquarters; children are free.) To the right is the Dewee house, restored to its 1790 appearance, and a barn and restored stable. Continuing ahead, on the right is the Isaac Potts house, circa 1770. The house was rented to General George Washington and served as his headquarters during the encampment. Twenty or more officers and staff members lived and worked in the house, directing the command and control of the entire Continental Army.

Turn right on the path, past the Valley Forge railroad station, built in 1913. Valley Creek joins the Schuylkill River just beyond the tracks. The train was a major route for tourism until the mid-twentieth century. Today, the tracks are used for freight only.

Continuing on the path, cross Park Road on a paved trail to walk past a group of log huts used by the Commander in Chief's guards. Fifty "life guards" were housed here; it was an honor to be chosen to protect General Washington, his head-quarters, and important papers. Continue straight ahead to the parking lot and your car at 6.8 miles.

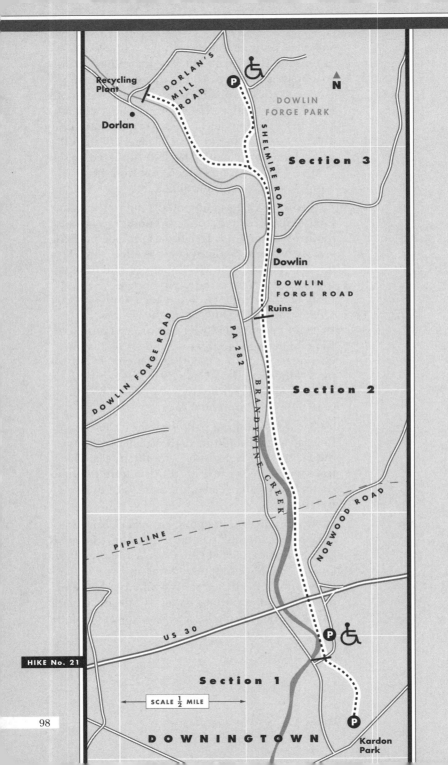

Recycling Plant

Dorlan

DORLAN'S MILL ROAD

P ♿

N

DOWLIN FORGE PARK

Section 3

SHELMIRE ROAD

Dowlin

DOWLIN FORGE ROAD

Ruins

PA 282

DOWLIN FORGE ROAD

BRANDYWINE CREEK

Section 2

NORWOOD ROAD

PIPELINE

US 30

HIKE No. 21

Section 1

SCALE ½ MILE

P ♿

P

DOWNINGTOWN

Kardon Park

No. 21

Struble Trail

For information only **Chester County Parks and Recreation Department**

c/o Springton Manor Farm, Box 455-K, Springton Road, Glenmoore, PA 19343; (610) 942-2450

Distance	6.2 miles (round trip from Kardon Park)
Elevation	30 feet
Time to hike	2½ hours
Surface	asphalt-paved trail, worn in places
Interesting features	remains of Dowlin Forge, built in 1785; follows the east branch of the scenic Brandywine Creek
Facilities	picnic tables and benches along trail and in Kardon Park; no rest rooms or water
Disability access	yes; see map for wheelchair-accessible parking
Hunting	no

Directions from US 202 near Exton:

To Kardon Park (Lions Trail)

1. drive west on US 30 (Exton–Downingtown) 5.0 miles
2. turn left (west) onto Business US 30, drive 2.0 miles
3. turn right (west) onto PA 282 at Downingtown
4. drive 0.1 mile to Kardon Park on right

Coordinates 40°00'39"N; 75°42'03"W

from Business US 30: To southern end of Struble Trail

1. drive west on PA 282 for 0.6 mile to Norwood Road
2. turn right; drive 0.2 mile on Norwood Road to the parking area on left just past the sign marking the start of the Struble Trail (40°01'00"N; 75°42'13"W)
3. follow the asphalt paved trail 50 feet to access the main trail

To northern end of Struble Trail

1. drive on PA 282 (west) 2.0 miles to Dowlin Forge Road
2. turn right, drive 0.5 mile to a stop sign (Shelmire Road)
3. continue straight ahead on Shelmire Road 0.6 mile, turn left into Dowlin Forge Park (40°02'52"N; 75°42'36"W)
4. follow an asphalt trail that runs parallel to Shelmire Road 2,000 feet to a wooden bridge to access the main trail

The Struble Trail, named after Chester County conservationist Bob Struble, was dedicated in October 1979. Built on Chester parklands on an abandoned railroad bed, it is a fine trail for bicyclists and wheelchair hikers as well as hikers on foot. From the southern end at Kardon Park to the recycling plant and return is 6.2 miles of fairly level terrain. This hike includes a variety of wildlife habitats—hardwood forests, marsh, and the Brandywine Creek. The fishing must be excellent, judging from the number of fishermen wading the river. Several old stone bridges cross feeder streams and are dated 1916.

The trail is described in three sections, proceeding north from Kardon Park.

Struble Trail

Section 1. Lions Trail

Kardon Park to Norwood Road, 0.5 mile

This part of the trail is 10 feet wide, smooth, and asphalt paved. Walk north along the edge of a small lake, with many birds: mallard and wood ducks, Canada geese, songbirds, even sea gulls. A sign warns against feeding the migratory waterfowl. Feeding them interferes with their migration patterns and could cause overpopulation at this site and disease. This sign was apparently being widely ignored at the time of our visits.

This section of the trail is accessible to wheelchair hikers at either end, on an asphalt path leading around iron gates. At the north end you will find the beginning of the Struble Trail at Norwood Road.

Section 2. Struble Trail (southern end)

Norwood Road to Dowlin Forge Road, 1.5 miles

As it passes through mixed hardwoods, with occasional marshy areas on either side, the trail parallels the east branch of the Brandywine Creek on the left. The trail is 8 feet wide, and though paved with asphalt, it is worn in places, with a slight uphill grade. At 1.0 mile look across the river to the Shady Acres Park. Note the many waterfowl along this part of the creek.

This section of the trail is accessible to the wheelchair hiker from Norwood Road, but not from Dowlin Forge Road (see directions above). There is no parking at Norwood Road. The trail continues north to Dowlin Forge Road.

Section 3. Struble Trail (northern end)

Dowlin Forge Road to Dorlan's Mill Road (at a recycling plant), 1.1 miles

Just after crossing Dowlin Forge Road you pass the ruins of Dowlin Forge on the right. Formerly called the Mary Ann Forge, it was built in 1785 by Samuel Hibberd and sold to John Dowlin in 1801. It was subsequently operated by three generations of Dowlins over a period of nearly a hundred years. A raceway (still evident) diverted water from the Brandywine Creek to the waterwheels beside the forge. Pig iron was heated by charcoal fires; then triphammers powered by the waterwheels pounded out the impurities. Further refining produced bar iron. Iron forges like this were forerunners of the methods of the modern steel industry; by 1791 there were thirty-seven such forges in existence in southeastern Pennsylvania. Mary Ann Forge was the earliest industrial site in Uwchlan Township, which later came to include a sawmill, gristmill, blacksmith shop, charcoal hearths, produce farm, boarding houses, dwellings, school, and company store. The community came to be called Dowlin Forge.

The trail continues to parallel the Brandywine Creek to your left. At 0.6 mile at a bend in the creek, a wooden boardwalk on your right crosses a marshy area, then leads to Shelmire Road. Cattails, rushes, and sedges provide food and cover to frogs and turtles. At 1.0 mile the worn-asphalt main trail changes to a gravel two-track and begins to level, then slopes slightly downhill to a recycling plant and an old stone bridge over the Brandywine.

This section of the trail is wheelchair accessible at the northern end from Dorlan's Mill Road, or from Shelmire Road (see directions above). It is not accessible at the southern end (Dowlin Forge Road).

After reaching the recycling plant at Dorlan's Mill Road at 3.1 miles, turn around and retrace your steps to return to your car at Kardon Park for a total of 6.2 miles.

White Clay Creek Preserve

No. 22

P.O. Box 172, Landenberg, PA 19350-0172
(610) 255-5415

Distance	4.1 miles
Elevation	25 feet
Time to hike	2 hours
Surface	blue-blazed woods road; sandy path
Interesting features	large sycamore, catalpa, and walnut trees; fine examples of early American architecture; hike from Pennsylvania to Delaware and back
Facilities	rest rooms, water, and picnic tables at visitors' centers in both Pennsylvania and Delaware
Disability access	no
Hunting	yes

Directions **from US 1 near the Maryland state line:**

1. take the Forrestville exit at PA 896, drive south 11.5 miles to South Bank Road
2. turn left onto South Bank Road (at a red barn on the right), drive 1.4 miles
3. park at the parking lot on the left just before the old stone meetinghouse

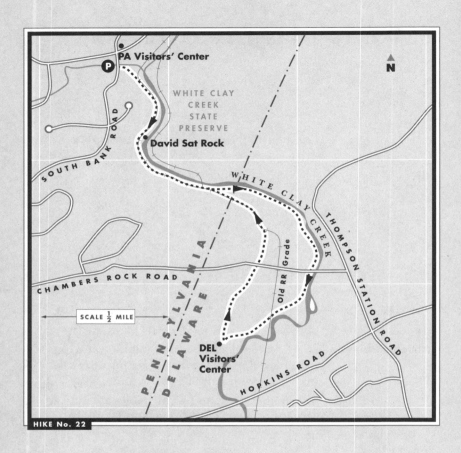

PA Visitors' Center

P

WHITE CLAY
CREEK
STATE
PRESERVE

David Sat Rock

SOUTH BANK ROAD

N

WHITE CLAY CREEK

THOMPSON STATION ROAD

CHAMBERS ROCK ROAD

Old RR Grade

SCALE ½ MILE

PENNSYLVANIA
DELAWARE

DEL
Visitors'
Center

HOPKINS ROAD

HIKE No. 22

Tucked away in the southeastern corner of the state and straddling the Delaware–Pennsylvania line, the White Clay Creek Preserve is scarcely used. It has been a part of the park system only since 1984, when the land was donated by the DuPont family to Pennsylvania and Delaware. This hike is easy, level walking, mostly along White Clay Creek.

The land was sold to William Penn in 1683 by Lenape Indian Chief Kekelappen. Chief Kekelappen lived in Opasiskunk, an "Indian town" that appeared on a survey map of 1699 at the confluence of the middle and eastern branches of White Clay Creek. Opasiskunk was a large settlement that covered several acres. Frequent flooding over the past two centuries have obliterated all evidence of this once important native settlement.

The visitors' center is the former London Tract Baptist Meeting House, built in 1729. The interior of the church, including wooden pews and furnishings, have been restored; the center also contains nature exhibits. In the stone-walled cemetery surrounding the meeting house are buried many of the area's oldest settlers. The churchyard is shaded by several magnificent northern catalpa and black walnut trees.

There are several interesting legends concerning this area, many featuring ghostly Indians and headless British soldiers from the Revolution. One story is about the early surveyors Mason and Dixon. It is said that in 1768, while Mason and Dixon were camped at the meeting house corner to survey the tangent points for Maryland and Pennsylvania, Mason was trying to make a chronometer. A baby wandered into the campsite and swallowed his invention. The child grew up to be a watchmaker and was eventually buried in the church graveyard. According to the legend, if you listen closely at the marble monument you can still hear the watch ticking. The writing on the old marker is no longer readable. Ask the park ranger at which headstone you should listen!

Across the street from the meeting house is the home of Dr. David Eaton. This classic example of a double-door Pennsylvania stone farmhouse is presently undergoing renovations, which are being carried out entirely by volunteers. Nearby is the Yeatman Mill House, of uncertain age, but probably the oldest dwelling in the area.

To begin the hike, cross South Bank Road and walk around a wooden painted gate, on a dirt woods road. A tributary of White Clay Creek is to your left. At 0.5 mile the tributary joins the 60-foot-wide White Clay Creek. Giant American sycamores (also called buttonwood trees) dominate the woods on the hillside to the right. Several faint fishing trails lead off to the left toward the creek.

There is a large outcropping at 0.6 mile and a rock just at the edge of the water, the David Sat Rock. Legend has it that a young boy named David sat on this rock for an entire day while his parents searched for him. Finally discovered at dusk, the boy had no explanation except that he was gripped by a compulsion to sit there. He was described as quite strange after this. Nothing more is known about him, but according to legend, sometimes just before dusk a figure of a young child can be glimpsed sitting on the rock, though the child disappears when approached.

Continue on the edge of the creek. Here we saw a great egret flying over the creek. This beautiful bird, with a wingspan of over 4½ feet, was once hunted for its feathers. Although the species has now recovered in numbers, it is still endangered by the destruction of habitat. It is at the northern limit of its range in Pennsylvania.

At 0.8 mile the woods road narrows to a trail. Another trail comes in from the right; this will be your return route. Bear left, toward the stream. At 1.2 miles note the remains of an old stone bridge at the creek bank as you enter Delaware. The trail becomes sandy (evidence of frequent flooding) and is lined by many large sycamore trees. At 1.4 miles you walk between a farm field and the stream. At 1.8 miles you will reach a parking lot and Chambers Rock Road. Cross the road, continuing on the blue-blazed trail.

The path continues to follow the creek's flood plain to the visitors' center in Delaware at 2.4 miles. At the edge of the parking lot, turn right on Tweeds Mill Road, a graveled road closed to traffic. Follow it until you cross Chambers Rock Road again at the edge of a cornfield. Here you reenter the mature hardwood forest.

You can identify the trees at White Clay Creek by their bark. Water-loving sycamores next to the creek have mottled white bark. Beech trees have smooth medium-gray bark, and the oaks have dark furrowed bark. At 3.2 miles you reenter Pennsylvania. Follow the trail to retrace your steps along the woods road to return to your car at 4.1 miles.

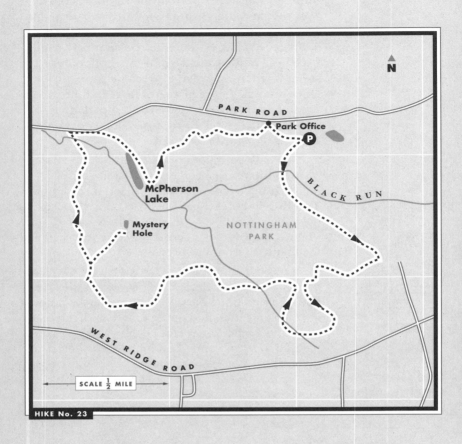

N

PARK ROAD

Park Office

P

B L A C K   R U N

McPherson Lake

Mystery Hole

NOTTINGHAM PARK

W E S T   R I D G E   R O A D

SCALE ½ MILE

HIKE No. 23

Nottingham Serpentine Barrens

Nottingham County Park

150 Park Road, Nottingham, PA 19362
(610) 932-9195

Distance	4.5 miles
Elevation	850 feet
Time to hike	2½ hours
Surface	gravel road, rocky and deeply rutted in places
Interesting features	outcroppings of rare, light green serpentine rock, found in just a few widely scattered places in the world; unique, desert-like habitat for many unusual plant species
Facilities	picnic areas with pavilions equipped with cooking grills and electrical outlets; playgrounds; fishing; camping; rest rooms and water
Disability access	1-mile fitness trail (gravel), pavilions, picnic facilities, and rest rooms accessible; trails, no
Hunting	no; the park is closed for controlled deer hunts once a year

Directions **from US 1 near the Maryland state line:**

1. take the Nottingham exit at PA 272, drive east 0.2 mile to Herr Drive
2. turn right onto Herr Drive and continue 0.3 mile

(continued)

to the stop sign at Old Baltimore Pike (the Herr Potato Chip factory is straight ahead)

3. turn right again onto Park Road, drive 0.8 mile (crossing over US 1) to the park on the left

4. turn left into the park, pull over to the right to a large trail sign and a box containing trail maps, turn immediately left and park near the park office; the Chrome Trail begins to the left of the rest rooms at the end of the parking lot

Coordinates 39°44'26"N; 76°02'11"W

North America has only three areas of serpentine outcrops: California and southern Oregon, the Gaspé Peninsula and western Newfoundland, and here in southeastern Pennsylvania and north-central Maryland. Serpentine has been quarried for building stone and used in many public buildings in Philadelphia. It has also been mined here for talc, asbestos, and chromium.

Located on an outcropping of serpentine stone, the Nottingham Barrens is a typical example of the way that vegetation is stunted because of the dry, acidic soil. From the mid-1800s until 1930, this area was the center of a feldspar- and chrome-quarrying industry. Mine openings and sinkholes throughout the park are evidence of this former mining activity. A small stream (Black Run) winds through the 651-acre park and acts as a dividing line between the uncultivated area and the developed recreation area.

Serpentine soils are low in essential nutrients and high in toxic metals, so much so that plants and trees that flourish in the surrounding deciduous forests will not grow in the barrens. Most barrens plants belong to species that are rare in southeastern Pennsylvania, though more common somewhere else. These include prairie grasses that live mainly in the West and Midwest and trees that are more common on the sandy Atlantic Coastal Plain.

Among the wildflowers, serpentine chickweed and mosspink in shades of light, medium, and dark pink bloom in April. Plain ragwort, with yellow, daisy-like flowers, blooms from May to July. These flowers are uncommon elsewhere but abundant here. The serpentine aster (*Aster depauperatus*) lives only on the barrens in Pennsylvania and Maryland, and nowhere else. It is in full bloom in September. Unusual birds like the bobwhite quail, barred owl, and whip-poor-will are found, as well as nineteen species of nesting warblers.

Begin walking southwest on the Chrome Trail, with small metal (yellow) blazes tacked to the trees. Stepping over Black Run at 0.15 mile, you enter the uncultivated area of the park. At 0.2 mile you reach an intersection with the Nature Trail at an outcropping of rock with a sign describing this unique ecosystem. Early farmers considered the area worthless for any type of agriculture and described it as barren—thus the name "barrens." The Chrome Trail turns left, joining the Doe Trail, which is marked with white triangles on the trees.

Wildflowers (bluets and moss pink in May) line the trail on both sides. The trees are mostly stunted pitch pine. Eastern cottontail rabbits, woodchucks (also called groundhogs), and many species of birds abound here as well.

At 0.7 mile turn right at the intersection with the red-blazed Buck Trail, which begins at a radio tower 500 feet farther on. Pass several 8" x 8" wood posts, which are used for orienteering (maps are available in the park office). You are walking through a rough and isolated part of the park, with mostly scrub pine and a few stunted oaks and shrubs.

Step over a small stream at 1.0 mile, following the red blazes. Note the many deer tracks along the stream. At the top of a hill with little vegetation except grasses, turn left on the orange-blazed Lonesome Pine Trail. The trees become even fewer and more stunted, and the rocks on the rutted road have a greenish tinge. At 1.2 miles turn right on an unblazed grassy fire road.

Pass a small grove of stunted beech saplings on the right. These thin out at 1.5 miles, where you reach an intersection with the Ridge Trail. Turn right and walk 500 feet; look carefully until you spot a faint path to the right, which leads to a sinkhole, 20 feet across and 25 feet deep. The sinkhole is the site of an abandoned chrome mine.

At 1.7 miles you will rejoin the Buck Trail (red blazes). Turn left. At 2.6 miles you will reach another trail intersection with six large boulders. The blue-blazed Mystery Hole Trail turns right. Follow it downhill for approximately 1000 feet from the intersection, and watch carefully for a trail to the left. The path leads to Mystery Hole, filled with water and lined with serpentine rock. An abandoned mine shaft, the steep rocky sides of the sinkhole make it hazardous to approach too closely.

Backtrack to the Buck Trail and turn right. As you continue, notice how the soil abruptly changes, along with the vegetation. One moment you are walking through a stunted pitch pine forest; the next, you are among ferns and hardwood trees—beech and a mixture of oak—no longer stunted. Skunk cabbage lines a stream to the right. Large nesting boxes on trees have been put up recently to attract wood ducks.

Continue ahead across a culvert and a grassy field, turning right at 3.4 miles to walk parallel to Park Road. Keeping a fenced show ring on your right, continue through a group of picnic tables to a dirt road. You will pass several types of bird nesting boxes. The ones next to the lake are part of a bluebird restoration project; however, many have been taken over by tree swallows. The boxes have been left in place, in the hope that the tree swallows nesting here will leave the bluebirds alone in other parts of the park. Other nesting boxes house purple martins. Turn left on the dirt road.

At 3.7 miles you reach McPherson Lake, a tranquil spot with benches on which to rest and enjoy the wildlife. We saw a family of Canada geese here—very protective parents and seven little, fluffy chicks. The Buck Trail ends at the southern end of McPherson Lake.

Turn left at a parking area for the lake, on a gravel road. You will pass a camping area, ball field, picnic pavilions, playground, rest rooms, and a 1-mile fitness trail.

At 4.5 miles you will reach the park office, which contains a small bookstore and nature exhibits, near the parking lot and your car.

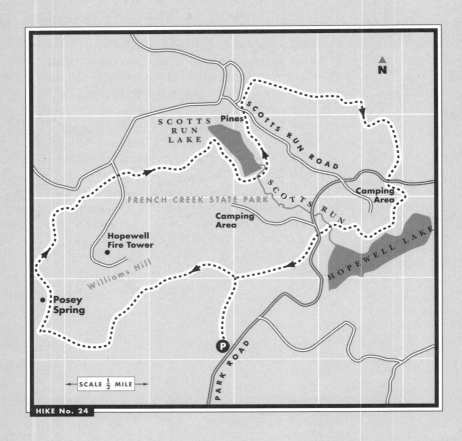

N

SCOTTS
RUN
LAKE

Pines

SCOTTS RUN ROAD

Camping
Area

FRENCH CREEK STATE PARK

SCOTTS RUN

Camping
Area

Hopewell
Fire Tower

HOPEWELL LAKE

Williams Hill

Posey
Spring

P

PARK ROAD

SCALE ½ MILE

HIKE No. 24

French Creek

No. 24

French Creek State Park
843 Park Road, Elverson, PA 19520
(610) 582-9680

Distance	8.0 miles
Elevation	980 feet
Time to hike	4½ hours
Surface	rocky woods trail
Interesting features	Scotts Run Lake; Hopewell Lake; remains of charcoal hearths; 6.3-mile section of the Horseshoe Trail
Facilities	rest rooms, water, picnic tables, and grills at picnic areas near lakes
Disability access	no
Hunting	yes

Directions **from US 202 near King of Prussia:**

1. drive west on US 422 for 30.5 miles
2. turn left (south) onto PA 82, drive 1.2 miles (into Birdsboro)
3. turn left (east) onto PA 724, drive 0.5 mile
4. turn right (south) onto PA 345, drive 6.5 miles
5. turn right onto South Entrance Road, drive 1.2 miles to Park Road
6. turn left onto Park Road for 0.3 mile to the parking lot on the right

French Creek State Park is one of the largest parks in southeastern Pennsylvania; it contains more than 30 miles of trails, including a section of the Horseshoe Trail. This historic trail runs more than 130 miles, from Valley Forge to the Appalachian Trail near Harrisburg, and has been recently rerouted through French Creek. A variety of habitats are found at French Creek, including densely wooded hillsides, streams, and wetlands, and many species of birds and other wildlife thrive here. In addition to hiking, French Creek State Park offers a permanent self-guided orienteering course, cross-country skiing, mountain biking, and two frisbee golf courses. (In frisbee golf, players take turns throwing a frisbee into cages on a 9 "hole" course.)

Begin hiking north from the parking lot. At 0.5 mile turn left on the yellow-blazed Horseshoe Trail. At 0.6 mile the trail joins the white-blazed Turtle Trail. The Horseshoe Trail was relocated through French Creek in 1995 onto the Turtle Trail; the new route removes the Horseshoe Trail from the eroded slopes of Williams Hill and adds 2.2 miles to the trail within the park.

Alongside the trail, look for 30- to 40-foot circular clearings, the remains of early nineteenth-century charcoal hearths. The owners of Hopewell Furnace, located a mile east of here, owned thousands of acres of the surrounding woodlands. Lumber was cut from the forest and hauled on sleds to the hearths, where it was charred to produce charcoal. The hot charcoal was then hauled to the village in metal-lined wagons to fire the blast iron furnace at Hopewell. The original forests, primarily of American chestnut, were essentially cleared. After the furnace was closed in 1883, the forest eventually regenerated, but with the mixture of oaks, hickories, and beeches found today.

At 3.0 miles the trail crosses the Fire Tower Road. Opened in the 1930s, Pennsylvania's fire towers were once important in fire prevention. The fire tower on Williams Hill in French Creek park was one of the last to be closed in Pennsylvania (in 1992). Although it has been closed to the public since 1995, the adjacent picnic area is open and can be reached by following the road for 0.5 mile to the top of Williams Hill.

The main trail is deeply rutted in some places and boggy where natural springs arise. In early spring you will find skunk cabbage in boggy areas along the streams as well as wildflowers, including violets and Jack-in-the-pulpits.

The Micajah Posey Spring on your left gives rise to a small unnamed stream.

On a hike in early spring we heard loud tapping very close by and looked up to see a woodpecker about the size of a crow. It was a pileated woodpecker, the largest of the woodpeckers, and not especially common in this area. They are noted for a prominent red crest and a loud ringing call. With the leaves off the trees, they are easily seen as well as heard tapping at dead trees in their search for insects.

After crossing the road to the fire tower, continue on the Horseshoe Trail to the 21-acre Scotts Run Lake at 4.0 miles. The trail follows the western edge of the lake to an earthen dam, then just below the dam crosses Scotts Run. Turn left here, following the Lenape Trail (yellow and green blazes) to enter a pine plantation at 4.4 miles.

You leave the quiet rows of pines at Scotts Run Road at 4.6 miles. Cross the road, following the yellow blazes uphill on a gravel road to a campground. At the top of the hill the Horseshoe Trail turns left at 4.8 miles. At this point you will leave the Horseshoe Trail to continue straight ahead on the blue-blazed Boone Trail.

At 5.5 miles the green-blazed Lenape Trail splits left toward Hopewell Village (see Hike 25). Turn right, following the Boone Trail at the edge of a parking lot. At 5.8 miles cross a campground road and at 5.9 miles, Park Road. At 6.0 miles turn right onto a yellow- and green-blazed trail as you approach 68-acre Hopewell Lake.

In the spring you are likely to hear the waterfowl at the lakes before you see them, competing for territory and raising young. Scotts Run and Hopewell lakes are favorite nesting spots for both resident and migratory birds, including geese, mallard ducks, and coots. Although there is hunting in some areas of the park, the lakes are off-limits, and the birds seem to realize they are safe.

As it is slightly warmer and protected from winds along the lake, you will also find flowering trees and shrubs in abundance in April and May, including pink and white dogwoods, azaleas, and Pennsylvania's state flower, mountain laurel.

At 6.8 miles cross a bridge over Scotts Run and then cross Park Road. At 7.5 miles watch carefully for a double yellow blaze and a yellow arrow on a tree. The trail to return to your car turns left (south) here. Return to your car at 8.0 miles.

Hopewell Village and Baptism Creek

No. 25

Hopewell Furnace National Historic Site

2 Mark Bird Lane, Elverson, PA 19520
(610) 582-8773

Distance	8.3 miles
Elevation	850 feet
Time to hike	4½ hours
Surface	rocky woods trail
Interesting features	early American iron-making community, Hopewell Village National Historic Site; Baptism Creek
Facilities	water and rest rooms at the visitors' center
Disability access	no
Hunting	yes

Directions **from US 202 near King of Prussia:**

1. drive west on US 422 for 30.5 miles
2. turn left (south) onto PA 82, drive 1.2 miles (into Birdsboro)
3. turn left (east) onto PA 724, drive 0.5 mile
4. turn right (south) onto PA 345, drive 5.0 miles
5. turn right into entrance, drive 0.3 mile to the parking lot and visitors' center

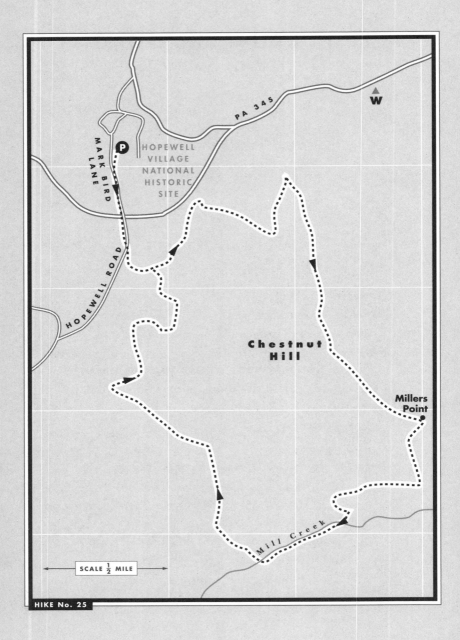

PA 345

W

P

MARK BIRD LANE

HOPEWELL VILLAGE NATIONAL HISTORIC SITE

HOPEWELL ROAD

Chestnut Hill

Millers Point

Mill Creek

SCALE ½ MILE

HIKE No. 25

Hopewell Furnace National Historic Site is the restoration of Hopewell village, an industrial community built in the eighteenth century for the manufacture of cast and wrought iron products. Cannon and shot produced here supplied the American revolutionaries. After the war the furnace turned to the production of stove plates, hardware, and horseshoes.

Behind the visitors' center lies the village, as it appeared in the 1820–1840 period—the imposing ironmaster's mansion, the cast house surrounding the furnace stack, the water wheel and blast machinery, charcoal hearths, blacksmith house, and many other restored buildings. During the summer, activities depicting village occupations are presented along the 0.75-mile walk through the village. (There is a fee of $2.00 for adults 17 years of age and older to visit the village; no charge to hike the trails.) Hopewell Village is open from 9:00 a.m. to 5:00 p.m. daily.

Walk down the steps behind the visitors' center to a gravel road—the village is just ahead. Turn left on the road through an apple orchard. Apple growing has also been part of Hopewell's history since the early 1800s. Over the years the orchard has been expanded to more than 250 trees. Twenty-five familiar and historic varieties of apples are grown. They ripen throughout September and October, and you can pick your own for a fee of $0.50 per pound. Spring is also a lovely time to visit, when the trees are in bloom all around the parking lot and the orchard.

Continue walking along Mark Bird Lane (access road), named after the first ironmaster at Hopewell, and cross PA 345 at 0.3 mile. Continue straight ahead on Hopewell Road between two fields, following the green-blazed Lenape Trail. Just after entering the woods, cross a tributary of Baptism Creek.

At 0.5 mile the green blazes leave the road to turn left into the woods; follow the blazes.

At a picnic shelter, following green and red blazes, bear left to again cross the tributary of Baptism Creek. Bear left (1.4 miles) at the trail intersection where the red-blazed Raccoon Trail turns right—that will be your return route. Continue uphill on the green-blazed Lenape Trail, ascending 380 feet to the Mill Creek Trail at 2.9 miles. Turn right on the Mill Creek Trail, following the white with red blazes.

The Mill Creek Trail, an old fire road, continues to the top of Chestnut Hill at 3.8 miles through mixed oaks and maples. Turn left, following the white with red blazes down a rocky woods road. The trail reaches Millers Point, a large rock formation, at 4.2 miles, and then descends even more sharply. Pass several intersections with other trails but remain on the Mill Brook Trail. As you descend, the trail becomes muddy in places, and you will note that several types of ferns predominate, including bracken, Christmas ferns, and ground pine.

Cross Mill Creek at 5.2 miles at an intersection with the red-blazed Raccoon Trail. Stay on the Mill Creek Trail. At 6.3 miles turn left on the Buzzard Trail, yellow with red blazes. The Buzzard Trail splits off just 0.1 mile ahead. Bear right, and then turn right again at 7.1 miles, staying on the Buzzard Trail. Shortly thereafter you cross several tributaries, and then Baptism Creek.

The creek was named "Baptizing Creek" by early members of the Lloyd Meeting House, whose minister performed baptisms in the creek. The congregation became the Bethesda Baptist Church in 1827. Their church served as a place of worship for the foundry workers of Hopewell. The restored church building stands just 0.2 mile from the creek on Bethesda Road. The tombstones surrounding the church, the earliest dating from May 1807, provide a history of the early workers at Hopewell.

After crossing several more feeder streams, you will come to a large yellow-poplar (tuliptree) on the right. Turn left on the red-blazed Raccoon Trail at 7.5 miles. Here you will see the ruins of an old farmhouse on the left. It serves as a reminder of the time when this area consisted of open fields, farms, and orchards. Stone walls are all that remain.

At 7.8 miles you reach the green-blazed Lenape trail; turn left, completing the loop begun at 1.4 miles. From here you retrace your steps along the Lenape Trail to return to your car at 8.3 miles.

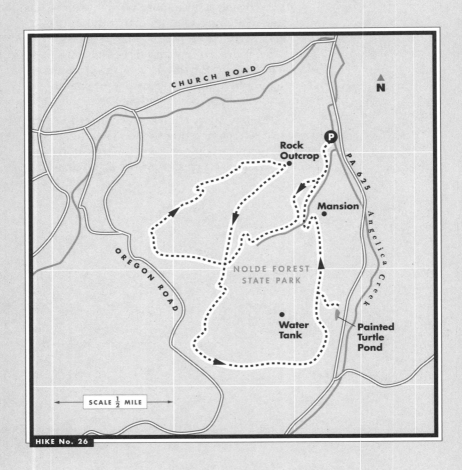

CHURCH ROAD

N

Rock
Outcrop

P

PA 625

Mansion

Angelica Creek

NOLDE FOREST
STATE PARK

OREGON ROAD

Water
Tank

Painted
Turtle
Pond

SCALE ½ MILE

HIKE No. 26

Nolde Forest

No. 26

Nolde Forest Environmental Education Center
R.D. 1, Box 392, Reading, PA 19607
(610) 775-1411

Distance	4.3 miles
Elevation	540 feet
Time to hike	2¼ hours
Surface	graveled road, woods trail
Interesting features	conifer plantation; mansion
Facilities	water, rest rooms at parking lot; rest rooms and picnic tables (no grills) at Boulevard and Cabin Hollow trails (1.0 mile)
Disability access	yes, on two short paved accessible trails located at the information kiosk and mansion areas; otherwise, no
Hunting	no

Directions **from US 202 near King of Prussia:**

1. drive west on US 422 (toward Pottstown–Reading) 39.0 miles
2. turn left (south) onto US 222, drive 0.6 mile
3. turn left (south) onto PA 625, drive 2.5 miles
4. turn right into Sawmill parking area

When hosiery baron Jacob Nolde first came to this area in the early 1900s, there were only poor-soil farms; most trees had been cut down for charcoal. However, he saw one white pine tree growing near what is now the sawmill and envisioned an entire conifer forest. By 1916 he had planted 500,000 evergreen trees, in cleared plantations or under-planted in the oak forest. These areas now provide a great variety of habitats, including hemlocks and pines both young and mature, mixed oak and hickory forest, and open meadows, especially along Angelica Creek. The diverse ecosystems encourage a great variety of animal and bird life.

Be sure to pick up a state park trail map at the information kiosk at the sawmill parking lot entrance. Note the many intersecting trails; there are even more in the park itself, as not all are shown on the map. It is possible to lay out many different hiking routes to suit the abilities of different hikers. The hike as described here includes a tumbling stream, the view from a rocky ridge, a small pond, the mansion, and the majestic conifer plantation that defines the forest.

Begin your hike at the edge of the parking lot, crossing Angelica Creek on a wooden bridge over the raceway for the nearby sawmill. The Watershed Trail follows Punches Run through thick hemlocks. At 0.7 mile you reach Mansion Road and cross Punches Run (40°16'45"N; 75°56'57"W). A little farther on, follow the Boulevard Trail on the north side of Punches Run.

The Watershed Trail continues to follow the stream on the south side, crossing the tiny stream several times. At 1.0 mile you reach an intersection with the Cabin Hollow Trail (40°16'24"N; 75°57'22"W) at a picnic grove. Continue to follow the trail on either side of Punches Run to the western edge of the park, ascending steadily from 400 to 750 feet.

The Watershed Trail ends at 1.8 miles (40°16'29"N; 75°57'41"W) at a springhouse. If you chose to hike on the Watershed Trail, turn right here and walk 60 feet to join the Boulevard Trail. The Boulevard Trail continues uphill to 840 feet, reaching a rock outcrop (40°16'48"N; 75°57'08"W) at 2.3 miles. In summer, views to the north and east are obscured by dense foliage. Return to the Boulevard Trail to complete the first loop at the Cabin Hollow Trail at 2.6 miles.

From this intersection follow the Cabin Hollow Trail, crossing Punches Run at 2.7 miles. At 2.9 miles you reach a clearing at the intersection of Middle Road and the Owl Loop Trail (40°16'09"N; 75°57'24"W) and the beginning of the stately pine forest. From here you can follow several routes to the mansion. If you take the Middle Road (a left turn), you will walk along row after row of planta-tion pine trees, and past a water tower (40°16'23"N; 75°57'09"W) that supplies water for the mansion.

Alternatively, you can continue straight ahead on the Owl Trail as shown on the map to an inter-section with the Buck Hollow Trail at 3.2 miles at the southern end of the park (40°16'05"N; 75°57'06"W). Turn left here, and after walking another 50 feet, bear left again through a dense hemlock forest.

At 3.5 miles you can glimpse the Painted Turtle Pond through the trees. Follow a short trail down to the edge of the pond (40°16'16"N; 75°57'01"W). The pond is a good place to rest and enjoy the wildlife found here, including frogs, woodpeckers, butterflies, and perhaps an Eastern painted turtle sunning himself on a plank in the water. Violets, skunk cabbage, and ferns grow along the edges of the pond in the spring; in July raspberries are abundant. A nearby meadow with bird nesting boxes attracts a variety of songbirds.

Return to the main trail, which continues to the McConnell Environmental Education Center (open weekdays only) at 3.8 miles. From here, you can walk along an accessible asphalt path to the stately Tudor-style mansion (40°16'37"N; 75°56'55"W), built in 1926 by Hans Nolde. The mansion looks like a medieval castle, complete with tower and balconies. A lovely garden adjoins the mansion, with tile fountains. Note the painted butterfly box set among the flowers. There are many elegant details to notice as you walk around this home—stained glass windows depicting biblical figures, a pine tree, and a pond; handwrought iron details; and the whimsical entrance to the children's quarters, complete with a cat boot scraper and wrought iron nursery figures on the door itself. The mansion has been converted to offices and is open from 8:00 a.m. to 4:00 p.m. Monday to Friday.

Return to Punches Run via the Mansion Road. Continue to the parking lot (40°16'52"N; 75°56'55"W) at 4.3 miles by retracing your steps on the Watershed Trail.

Not all the trails are clearly marked and their names are changed frequently, so you may discover that you are not on the trail you thought you were. Nevertheless, you are unlikely to get truly lost. The park is bordered by Angelica Creek and PA 625 on the east and south, Oregon Road on the west, and Church Road on the north. Trails leading downhill will take you to either Punches Run, which bisects the park, or Angelica Creek.

This hike is especially suited to navigate with GPS (global positioning system) technology, using the landmark positions we have provided. Think in terms of destinations—first Punches Run, then the rock outcrop, the pine forest, the water tower, Painted Turtle Pond, and the mansion—as you update your position and navigate your route.

No. 27

Daniel Boone Homestead

400 Daniel Boone Road, Birdsboro, PA 19508
(610) 582-4900

Distance	1.5 miles
Elevation	20 feet
Time to hike	1 hour
Surface	graveled road, woods trail
Interesting features	typical eighteenth-century farm; historic buildings; lake
Facilities	water, rest rooms, picnic tables, and benches at many locations
Disability access	no
Hunting	no

Directions   **from US 202 near King of Prussia:**

1. take US 422 (west towards Pottstown), drive 30.1 miles
2. turn right onto Daniel Boone Road (SR 2041), drive 0.7 mile
3. turn left at park entrance road, following the signs to the visitors' center

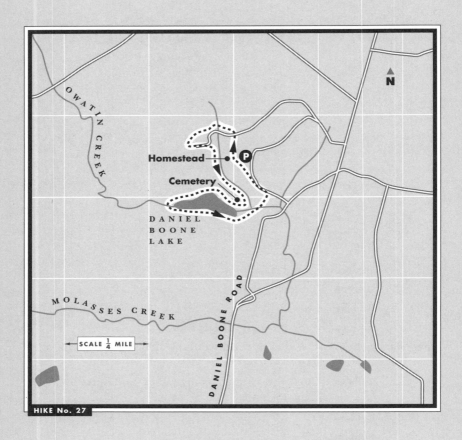

OWATIN CREEK

Homestead

Cemetery

DANIEL BOONE LAKE

N

P

MOLASSES CREEK

SCALE $\frac{1}{4}$ MILE

DANIEL BOONE ROAD

HIKE No. 27

Daniel Boone, American frontiersman, became famous for his leadership in settling the Kentucky wilderness in the late 1700s. He was born in this farmhouse near Reading, Pennsylvania, on November 2, 1734, to English Quaker parents. Daniel was the sixth child, one of eleven, and he was raised on this typical farm of the time. When Daniel was only fifteen and a half years old, the family moved to North Carolina for economic and perhaps religious reasons; his father had been "read out of meeting" for allowing another son to marry a non-Quaker.

Between 1775 and 1783 Daniel Boone led efforts to open up the Kentucky frontier to settlers and to defend them against Indian raids. He returned to his boyhood home in Pennsylvania twice, in 1782 and 1788, already a legendary pioneer and Indian fighter.

The farm was purchased from the Boones in 1750 by William Maugridge, a Boone relative, and was sold again in 1770 to John DeTurk, a Pennsylvania German. Since 1938 the Daniel Boone Homestead has been a state-owned historic site, administered by the Pennsylvania Historical and Museum Commission.

Begin at the visitors' center, which contains exhibits, a slide show, publications, and tickets for a tour of the farmhouse. The center and trails are open Tuesday to Saturday 9:00 a.m. to 5:00 p.m.; and Sunday, noon to 5:00 p.m.; closed Mondays. There is a fee for a guided tour of the farmhouse ($4.00 for adults; $2.00 for children 6–12; and $3.00 for senior citizens); there is no charge to visit other buildings or trails.

From the parking lot walk behind the visitors' center through an apple orchard to the Boone House, straight ahead. Turn right on the gravel path past several outbuildings. The blacksmith shop and large red barn are straight ahead. The barn was built on the foundations of the original DeTurk barn and contains implements, tools, and wagons from the period. Sheep, chickens, and geese are kept in pens alongside the barn.

Walk up stone steps and turn left on a gravel service road, along a four-rail fence. Horses graze in a field to your left. As the road bends left, continue straight ahead across a grassy field, to the log Bertolet House. This house was built in 1737 and relocated here in 1968. It is a fine example of eighteenth-century Pennsylvania German architecture. Although it is not open to the public, you can look in the door to view the massive stone fireplace open to the kitchen, the wide plank floors, and wooden implements. The adjoining combination bakehouse–smokehouse is also from the period. The clay tile roofs on both structures were a common roofing material in the German communities.

Return to the gravel road and continue past a springhouse to the Bertolet sawmill. The mill was built around 1810; it was moved to this site in 1972. Turn right at the mill dam and walk up a few steps to the DeTurk cemetery. Continue straight ahead on a narrow path along Daniel Boone Lake. This small scenic lake provides a nesting place for many varieties of waterfowl. Besides Canada geese, we saw a flock of domesticated white-fronted geese, identified by their orange legs and unusual call. Spring flowers flourish along the edge of the lake.

Continue to the upper reaches of the lake, bearing left to cross Owatin Creek on a footbridge. Mixed oak and hickory forest gives way to a meadow and picnic tables on the other side. Pass a utility building and a lodge, cross another bridge to a picnic grove, and return via a gravel path to the Boone House. Turn right through the apple orchard to the parking lot and your car at 1.5 miles.

Green Lane Reservoir

No. 28

Green Lane Reservoir Park

P.O. Box 249, Hill Road, Green Lane, PA 18054
(215) 234-4863

Distance	5.2 miles
Elevation	280 feet
Time to hike	2½ hours
Surface	rocky multi-use trail
Interesting features	260 species of birds sighted (pick up bird checklist at park office); interpretive nature trail; large reservoir; fishing
Facilities	water, rest rooms, picnic tables, and grills at the visitors' center
Disability access	no
Hunting	no

Directions **from US 202 near King of Prussia:**

1. take US 422 (west toward Pottstown), drive 8.2 miles to PA 29

2. turn right (north) onto PA 29 (toward Collegeville), drive 14.6 miles to Hill Road (SR 1037), turn left

3. continue for 1.2 miles to park entrance road, turn right and drive 0.5 mile to parking lot

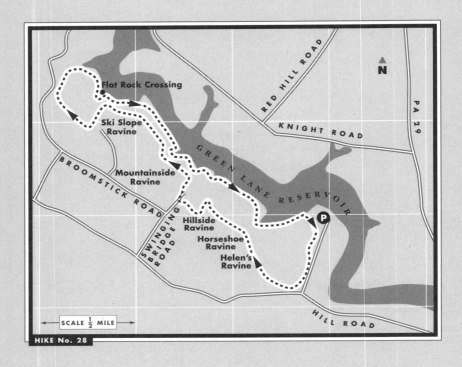

Flat Rock Crossing

Ski Slope
Ravine

RED HILL ROAD

N

PA 29

KNIGHT ROAD

GREEN LANE RESERVOIR

BROOMSTICK ROAD

Mountainside
Ravine

SWINGING BRIDGE ROAD

Hillside
Ravine

P

Horseshoe
Ravine

Helen's
Ravine

SCALE ½ MILE

HILL ROAD

HIKE No. 28

The primary purpose of the Green Lane Reservoir is to supply water for the city of Philadelphia and suburbs. However, it is also a relatively little-known and underdeveloped park in the far reaches of northern Montgomery County, consisting of 2,491 acres of woods and fields, including the 805-acre lake. Twenty miles of multi-use trails through a variety of natural environments provide spectacular views and challenges for hikers, bikers, and horse riders.

At the end of the parking lot look for a sign for the Nature Trail. Walk past a small outdoor classroom to a trail marked with blue ribbons tied to trees. Turn left at a trail register to walk through mixed hardwoods. The Whitetail Trail, an interpretive nature trail, runs concurrently with the blue multi-use trail. Post markers, some in disrepair, mark points of interest; these are described in a booklet that you can obtain at the park office. At 0.4 mile turn right onto the park entrance road. Follow the blue ribbons, to reenter the woods at a stand of red cedars.

The cedars give way to a mature mixed hardwood forest of white, red, and black oak, shagbark hickory, and beech, with a scattering of hemlock at lower elevations. At 0.6 mile you will come to a huge white oak, perhaps 600 years old, at post 18. The trail continues up and down a series of ravines and intermittent streams—Helen's Ravine, Hillside Ravine, Horseshoe Ravine. At 1.6 miles you reach Swinging Bridge Road, an old gravel road. Turn right, following the blue ribbons. After passing Mountainside Ravine, at 2.4 miles, you come to a sign for a "turn around." (You may take a cutback here by turning right, shortening your hike to 4.2 miles total.)

At 2.7 miles you reach Rock Falls at a "Y" in Ski Slope Ravine. From here, the trail turns back at a road and descends to the edge of the reservoir. Continue to the aptly named Flat Rock crossing, where layers of shale slick with moss line the stream bed. The trail then ascends quite steeply to a splendid view of the reservoir from the top of a hill.

Follow the trail as it descends to follow the edge of the reservoir closely, around coves and inlets. We saw a family of mallard ducks paddling at the edge of the water here. Herons and Canada geese are also often seen along the shoreline. Deer are abundant and seem to have little fear of humans. Turkeys are attracted to the acorns and beech nuts in the denser stands of mature hardwoods. At 5.2 miles you reach the trail register, the edge of the parking lot, and your car.

To hear a recorded message on trail conditions and special park activities, you may call an information line—(215) 234-2877. There are plans to further develop the Green Lane Reservoir Park, including additional boat launches, campsites, expanded day use, and extension of the trail system. For now, Green Lane and its trails are quiet, peaceful, and little used.

Peace Valley

No. 29

Peace Valley County Park

230 Creek Road, Doylestown, PA 18901
(215) 822-8608

Distance	4.0 miles
Elevation	180 feet
Time to hike	2 hours
Surface	paved asphalt trail for the first 0.9 mile; then woods trail, fairly easy walking; two stream crossings on stepping stones
Interesting features	365-acre Lake Galena, scenic streams; many deer (no hunting); waterfowl habitat; diverse habitats of fields, woods, ponds, and streams; more than 260 species of birds, including egrets, great blue herons, and bald eagles
Facilities	rest rooms at trailhead and at nature center; water at nature center; picnic tables and benches at several locations
Disability access	yes, for the first 0.9 mile, to the nature center
Hunting	no

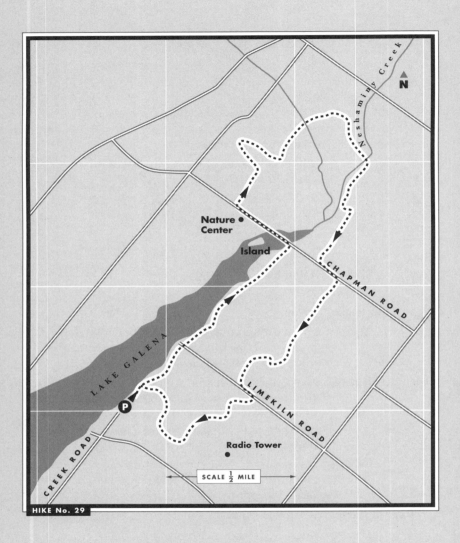

Nature
Center ●

Island

LAKE GALENA

Neshaminy Creek

CHAPMAN ROAD

LIMEKILN ROAD

P

Radio Tower
●

CREEK ROAD

N

SCALE ½ MILE

HIKE No. 29

Directions **from US 202 near New Britain:**

1. in Chalfont turn north on PA 152 (North Main Street), drive 0.2 mile

2. turn right on Park Avenue (SR 1006)—name changes to Callowhill Road

3. drive 1.8 miles on Park and Callowhill, turn right at stop sign onto Creek Road

4. drive 1.9 miles to a parking area at the end of the road

Coordinates 40°19'46"N; 75°10'50"W

Peace Valley Park contains a wide variety of natural habitats, including meadows, cultivated and over-grown fields, streams, marshes, stands of conifers, and second-growth woods. Lake Galena, 365 acres in size, is home to many varieties of waterfowl. In fact, more than 260 species of all types of birds have been recorded here—80 percent of the species found in eastern Pennsylvania. In addition, because there is no hunting, the deer are rather tame. On a recent hike we spotted no less than five groups of deer.

Begin the hike at the end of the parking lot by walking along the lake on an asphalt road. There are several picnic tables beside the lake. At 0.3 mile follow an arrow painted on the road to bear right on a newly paved asphalt trail. Here, small mixed hardwoods are interspersed with cornfields. Spruce and pine trees have been planted in several open areas.

At 0.5 mile you will find a short path to a bird blind overlooking a protected wildlife conservation area. Cormorant Island ahead is a favorite breeding area for several pairs of nesting waterfowl.

As you continue you will reach a T intersection with Chapman Road at 0.6 mile. Turn left to walk across a bridge over the north branch of Neshaminy Creek, which empties into the eastern end of the lake. This bridge is subject to flooding when the water level rises in the spring.

At 0.9 mile you reach the Peace Valley Nature Center, where you may pick up maps and view exhibits on wildlife of special interest to children. Saturday bird walks and environmental education programs are offered. There are also a bird feeding station, pond, and additional nature trails behind the center. The nature center is open Tuesday to Sunday from 9:00 a.m. to 5:00 p.m.

Pick up the Indian Path at the edge of the parking lot. No bicycles or pets are allowed on this section. It is graveled for the first 0.5 mile. You will encounter many crisscrossing trails, with occasional signs indicating the names of some. Blue blazes mark many trails; sometimes turns are indicated by three rocks stacked on top of each other. The trail can be hard to follow, especially if the ground is covered with leaves or snow. To take the longest route through the park, simply bear left at all the trail intersections. A right turn will lead back to the nature center.

At 2.2 miles you reach the north branch of the Neshaminy Creek. It is about 30 feet wide but can be crossed on stepping stones. You may get your feet wet when the water level is high, however. On the other side turn right on the Upper Woods Trail, marked by blue blazes. At the next trail intersection turn left at a sign for the Morning Bird Walk Trail, leaving the woods to walk along the edge of a cornfield.

You reach Chapman Road and a parking lot with picnic tables at 2.5 miles. Turn left to walk 500 feet along the single-lane road, then turn right on a gravel road closed to traffic. After walking another 200 feet turn left onto the Spring House Trail, marked with white blazes. At 2.7 miles you reach a stone springhouse after passing the ruins of an old stone farmhouse and barn. This area is low and swampy, but the trail has been recently improved with planks and stepping stones. There is a bird blind and viewing platform overlooking a wildlife preservation area.

Continue to Limekiln Road. Turn left to walk 500 feet along up the single-lane road; turn right onto a blue-blazed trail. The trail continues through second-growth woodland. At 3.7 miles you reach an abandoned farm pond, where you will pick up a white-blazed trail. At 3.9 miles you leave the woods to come into an open field, with Lake Galena straight ahead. Your car is to the left at the parking lot across the field, at 4.0 miles.

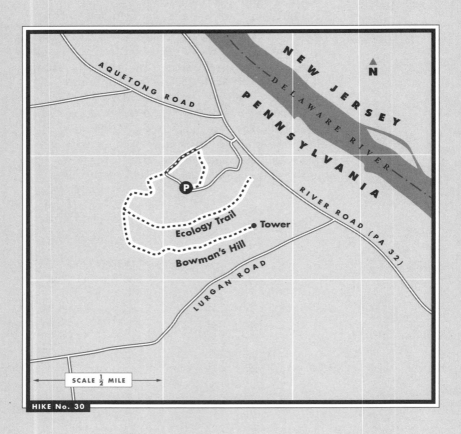

AQUETONG ROAD

NEW JERSEY

PENNSYLVANIA

DELAWARE RIVER

N

RIVER ROAD (PA 32)

P

Ecology Trail

● Tower

Bowman's Hill

LURGAN ROAD

SCALE $\frac{1}{2}$ MILE

HIKE No. 30

No. 30

Bowman's Hill State Wildflower Preserve

For information only **Washington Crossing Historic Park**

P. O. Box 103, Washington Crossing, PA 18977
(215) 493-4076

Distance	3.4 miles
Elevation	410 feet
Time to hike	2¼ hours
Surface	graveled paths, rocky trails
Interesting features	wildflower preserve, containing 1,500 herbaceous plants, famous for native wildflower collections; open all year, but best time for spring wildflowers is May; Bowman's Hill Tower
Facilities	picnic area near the highway entrance; no pets or picnicking within preserve; rest rooms at visitors' center and at Bowman's Hill Tower; benches along trails
Disability access	1,000-foot Woods Edge Trail (loop) is asphalt-paved and wheelchair accessible; wheelchair available on loan at the visitors' center; accessible parking at trailhead
Hunting	no

from I-95 near Levittown:

1. take exit 31 (New Hope), drive north on Taylorsville Road for 5.1 miles

2. turn left (north) onto PA 32 (River Road), drive 2.4 miles to the Bowman's Hill Wildflower Preserve on the left

3. drive past a picnic area and pavilion, press a button to open the gate to enter and continue to the visitors' center and parking lot

Coordinates 40°19'43"N; 74°56'37"W

The Bowman's Hill Wildflower Preserve is part of Washington Crossing Historic Park, the site of the famous crossing of the Delaware River by George Washington on Christmas Day, 1776. The wildflower preserve, located on the other side of River Road 4 miles from the park headquarters, is dedicated to the preservation and protection of native wildflowers, ferns, trees, and shrubs, which here grow in natural settings along twenty-six trails. It is open 9:00 a.m. to 5:00 p.m. daily; noon to 5:00 p.m. Sunday; closed major holidays. Bowman's Hill Tower, built to commemorate a famous lookout of the American Revolution, is an additional attraction.

Begin at the visitors' center, where you can pick up a free trail map and blooming guide to the plants. (There are two versions, one for spring and early summer and one for late summer and fall.) Individual trails are sponsored by various local garden clubs. Most are fairly short, from 200 to 2,000 feet long. All are marked with an entrance sign, directional arrows at turns, and painted keystone markers every 50 feet. The guide lists the plants by the name of the trail and the footage from the trail's start; specific plant locations can be determined by estimating from the nearest keystone marker. The guide also lists the common and scientific names, the color of the flower, and blooming times by month. Trees, shrubs, ferns, and grasses are also listed.

The birds in the preserve are as diverse as the flowers. Be sure to pick up a free bird guide, which lists them by the best time of year to observe them, their frequency of occurrence, and resident or migratory status. The visitors' center contains a large glassed-in observation area overlooking a bird feeding station, and downstairs is a collection of birds, eggs, and nests. Besides the extensive wildflower collection, on this hike you are also likely to see several species of butterflies as well as turtles, frogs, and insects, especially at the pond and creek.

The mile-long Penn's Woods Tree Trail leads through a 9-acre arboretum within the preserve. It is a living collection of Pennsylvania's native trees, sixty-eight in all; each is labeled with its common and scientific names. This is a great place to learn to identify native trees.

The names of the Bluebell Trail, Holly Walk, Medicinal Trail, and Azaleas-at-the-Bridge Trail are descriptive of the plants on these trails. On the Azalea Trail look for the state tree of Pennsylvania, a 240-year-old Canadian hemlock. The Ecology Trail leads 0.8 mile through deciduous forest to Pidcock Creek, becoming rocky and somewhat overgrown. The creek is too deep to cross easily; you will need to backtrack to return.

The preserve is entirely encircled with a 2-mile-long, 10-foot high chain link fence erected to protect the plants from the abundant deer in the area. Ten percent of the plants growing in the preserve are rare or endangered in Pennsylvania; a few are on the federal list of endangered species. The fence was erected in 1992 in the belief that it would be the only long-term practical means of protecting the collection. There are even wooden stake fences at the entrance and exit of the creek. However, even this does not seem completely effective; we saw fresh deer tracks along the creek.

Walk south up the road through the park and push open the gate leading to the Bowman's Hill Tower. It is a 0.9-mile walk from the visitors' center to the tower. The last 0.4 mile is on an asphalt road open to one-way motor traffic. Near the top of the steep climb you pass on the left the grave of Jonathan Pidcock, a soldier of the Revolution. Bowman's Tower, a 110-foot stone observation tower, was built in 1930 to commemorate this lookout of the American Revolution. It commands an impressive 14-mile view of the Delaware River valley. The tower is open from April to November. You can take an elevator most of the way up; an additional twenty-three steps lead to the top. There is a charge to visit the tower; adults: $4.00; youths (6–12): $2.00; children under 6: free; adults over 60: $3.00. Tickets are good at all the historic buildings at Washington Crossing Historic Park.

The peak time for spring flowers is mid-April through May, but summer and fall flowers are in bloom till frost. You can easily design your own walk through the preserve, depending on the time of year and what's in bloom. If you take the longer trails, you will walk 3 to 4 miles, but you may find it takes more time than you expected as you stop to enjoy the flowers and plants along the way.

Tohickon Valley

No. 31

Ralph Stover State Park

6011 State Park Road, Pipersville, PA 18947
(610) 982-5560

Distance	4.5 miles
Elevation	330 feet
Time to hike	2¼ hours
Surface	rocky woods trail
Interesting features	rock climbing; white-water rafting; scenic views
Facilities	water, rest rooms, picnic tables, and grills
Disability access	no
Hunting	no

Directions **from US 202 near New Britain:**

1. drive north on PA 611 for 3.6 miles
2. turn right onto Connector "A" Road, then drive 0.2 mile to a T intersection
3. turn left onto Point Pleasant Pike (SR 1006), drive 6.2 miles to a stop sign
4. turn left onto Tohickon Hill Road, drive 0.9 mile
5. turn right onto State Park Road (SR 1009), drive 1.1 miles
6. turn right into parking lot, just before the bridge over Tohickon Creek

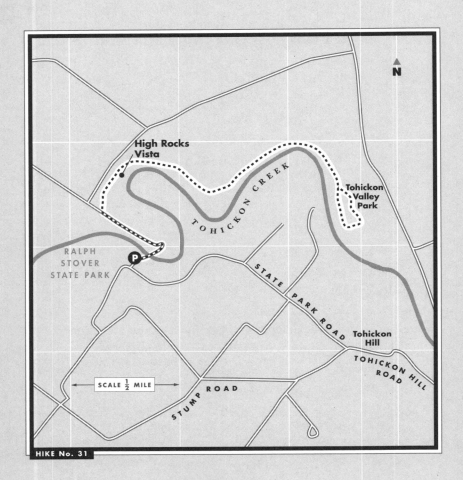

High Rocks
Vista

TOHICKON CREEK

Tohickon
Valley
Park

RALPH
STOVER
STATE PARK

P

STATE PARK ROAD

Tohickon
Hill

TOHICKON HILL
ROAD

N

SCALE ½ MILE

STUMP ROAD

HIKE No. 31

This hike, from Ralph Stover State Park to Tohickon Valley Park and back, takes the hiker past spectacular views from a high rocky ridge overlooking Tohickon Creek. The creek was aptly named by the Leni Lenape Indians *To-Hick-Hanne*, meaning "deer bone creek." You will have many opportunities to see deer and other wildlife here.

Begin the hike at the parking lot by crossing the 100-foot-wide Tohickon Creek over a bridge closed to vehicular traffic. Next to the bridge is a white-water boat launch area. When high-water conditions exist, Tohickon Creek offers a challenging course for closed-deck canoes and kayaks.

On the other side of the creek turn left and follow the one-lane Stover Park Road uphill past several private homes. At 0.4 mile the road intersects the High Rocks Trail. Turn right, following infrequent white blazes through a mixed hardwood forest. At 0.5 mile you reach the first of four scenic overlooks. The Argollite, Balcony, Cedar and Doan's overlooks provide spectacular views of a horseshoe curve of Tohickon Creek. Called High Rocks Vista, this is a popular site for rock climbing. Signs warn that only experienced rock climbers should attempt the 200-foot-high sheer rock face. Many injuries and deaths have occurred here. The trail has a safety fence along the side to protect the unwary hiker from a misstep. Still, young children, especially adventurous and mischievous ones, should probably not come along on this hike.

Continue on the High Rocks Trail on the eastern flank of the high ridge, with Tohickon Creek 200 to 250 feet below. You will encounter many intersecting trails; the blazes are now white with red circles. At 0.9 mile you begin a gradual descent toward the creek. Note the remains of a stone fence to your left. At 1.5 miles you reach a grove of hemlock trees and begin to climb again to the top of the ridge. At 1.8 miles step over a small stream that feeds into the Tohickon.

At 2.0 miles you reach a T intersection at the Tohickon Valley Park, where you will begin to follow a loop. The white blazes with red circles direct the visitor toward some picnic tables. Instead, turn right to follow the trail toward the stream. At 2.1 miles you reach a one-lane asphalt road, Park Road. Turn left to walk uphill past stone fences on the left and a pool on the right. Reach a parking area with playground equipment, picnic tables, grills, and water. At 2.2 miles turn left on a wooden footbridge toward the picnic area through the remains of several stone fences, and through a grassy area to the gravel campground road. Turn left, and at 2.5 miles turn left again past a water pump to complete the small loop you began at 2.0 miles.

From here, you retrace your steps on the High Rocks Trail to return to your car at 4.5 miles at the Ralph Stover State Park.

Lake Nockamixon No.32

Nockamixon State Park

1542 Mountain View Drive, Quakertown, PA 18951
(215) 538-2151

Distance	5.6 miles
Elevation	420 feet
Time to hike	3 hours
Surface	equestrian trails
Interesting features	panoramic views of 1,450-acre Lake Nockamixon from a high ridge; varied habitats; cedar forest
Facilities	no
Disability access	no
Hunting	yes

Directions **from US 202 near New Britain, PA:**

1. drive north on PA 611 for 14.5 miles to PA 412
2. turn left (north) onto PA 412, drive 0.5 mile to PA 563
3. turn left (south) onto PA 563, drive 6.0 miles to parking area on the left

Coordinates 40°26'25"N; 75°15'37"W

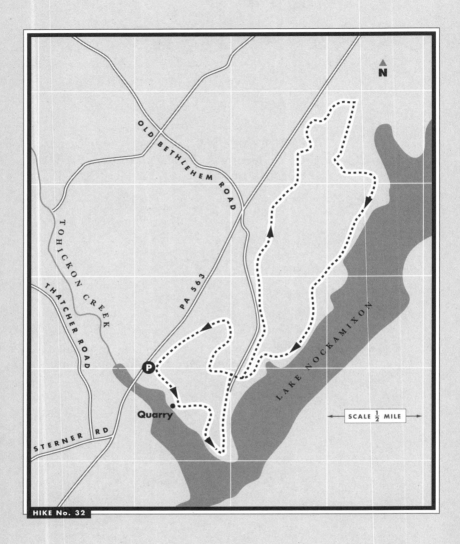

N

OLD BETHLEHEM ROAD

TOHICKON CREEK

THATCHER ROAD

PA 563

P

Quarry

STERNER RD

LAKE NOCKAMIXON

SCALE ½ MILE

HIKE No. 32

Lake Nockamixon was created in 1974 by the Department of Environmental Resources as the centerpiece of the Nockamixon State Park. However, soon the lake collected all sorts of pollutants. By 1981 a Pennsylvania Department of Environmental Resources study found traces of the pesticides chlordane and DDD (a residue of DDT) in the lake sediment, as well as polychlorinated biphenyls or PCBs, which are known to be carcinogenic. In response to the pollution, which had made the lake smelly and all but unusable, in 1983 Bucks County joined the Environmental Protection Agency's Clean Lakes Program. The county received nearly $500,000 in state and federal grants to clean up the lake.

A study found that 50 percent of the pollution was coming from the old Quakertown sewage treatment plant, built in 1926. Another 28 percent—nitrogen, phosphorus, and silt—came from runoff of fertilizer, manure, and soils from surrounding farms. The remainder came from malfunctioning septic systems nearby and storm runoff.

In response to the study, a $13 million sewage treatment plant was built in Quakertown in 1985, with federal grants covering 80 percent of the costs. The following year the county began a program to aid farmers in controlling runoff. Twenty-eight projects were begun on grain, sheep, horse, and dairy farms; each year these have prevented an estimated 10,000 tons of pollution from reaching the lake.

Today, tests show that the phosphorus pollution levels are about half what they were in 1981. The lake is clean, clear, and unpolluted. It supports a variety of fish species and provides recreational opportunities for people as well. This hike takes you through old hardwood forests, fields, and meadows; you will walk through second-growth woods, a cedar forest, and an old pine plantation, and along the edge of the now clean and unpolluted lake.

Begin at a metal gate and walk south on a gravel road. At a stone pillar at 500 feet, turn left on a trail through mixed hardwoods. Follow the signs of a rider on horseback tacked 8 feet high on trees. You will pass the remains of stone foundations of homesteads and farms.

At 0.4 mile you will reach the top of a ridge overlooking the lake and a large, partially water-filled amphitheater, the old Tohickon Quarry. Hornfels was mined at the quarry from 1936 to 1972, when the land was acquired by the state. The steep walls of the quarry were graded for safety. Hornfels is a tough, dark bluish-gray, fine-grained metamorphic rock that was used for a variety of construction purposes, including road-stone. There are only a few still-exposed ledges of the mineral remaining; the quarry now is filled with runoff and water lillies.

Bear left around the quarry, following the signs and arrows for the equestrian trail. The trail continues to ascend through small pines and shrubby undergrowth. At 0.6 mile the vegetation thins out and offers a full panoramic view of the 1,500-acre lake on the right.

At 0.7 mile several unmarked trails come in from the left. Continue straight ahead on the trail. Several bird nesting boxes and many raspberry canes line the trail. At 0.8 mile the trail slopes down to the edge of the lake. You enter an unusual forest of cedars—the cedar is a shrubby evergreen tree that grows up to 30 feet high. Cross an old asphalt launch road at 1.0 mile to a young hardwood forest of maple and birch.

The trail is no doubt very muddy for several days after a rain. At 1.2 miles you will reach a parking lot. Turn left and walk along a one-lane paved road, passing a marker for a horse trail on the left. At the top of a rise at 1.8 miles an equestrian trail crosses the road. At this point you may turn left to walk 0.4 mile through hardwoods to return to your car, for a total hike of 2.2 miles.

Turn right through mixed hardwoods, dense underbrush, pine plantations, and fields. At 2.0 miles you will reach a trail intersection; the trail that lies straight ahead will be your return route. Bear left uphill through a meadow. The trail is fairly well marked with yellow ribbons and signs for the horse trail. At a T intersection turn right (south) to head back along the edge of the lake. Walk through breaks in several stone fences, 3 feet high, evidence of farming prior to the creation of the lake. Spring and fall are the best times to see migrating shorebirds and waterfowl. Many, such as grebes, herons, and ducks of all types nest here as well. At 5.0 miles you will complete the loop you began at 2.0 miles.

Retrace your steps to the asphalt road at 5.2 miles. Cross the road to head uphill through the woods (passing a trail coming in from the left 100 feet from the road). At 5.6 miles you return to your car.

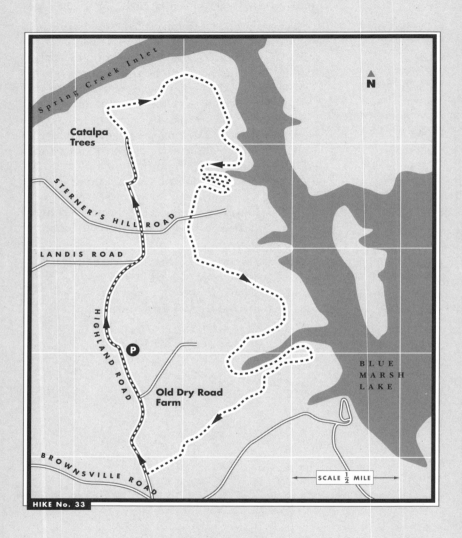

Spring Creek Inlet

N

Catalpa
Trees

STERNER'S HILL ROAD

LANDIS ROAD

HIGHLAND ROAD

P

Old Dry Road
Farm

BROWNSVILLE ROAD

BLUE
MARSH
LAKE

SCALE ½ MILE

Old Dry Road Farm

No. 33

For information only **Blue Marsh Lake Project**

U.S. Army Corps of Engineers, Philadelphia
District, RD #1, Box 1239, Leesport, PA 19533
(610) 376-6337

Distance	6.3 miles
Elevation	580 feet
Time to hike	3 hours
Surface	woods trail; farm roads
Interesting features	wetlands; rolling farmland; lake
Facilities	none
Disability access	no
Hunting	yes

Directions **from US 202 near King of Prussia:**

1. drive west on US 422 (toward Pottstown–Reading) 42.4 miles to the Bern Road exit near Reading, turn right
2. at bottom of exit ramp turn left onto State Hill Road, drive 4.0 miles to a T intersection
3. turn left onto Brownsville Road, drive 1.7 miles
4. turn right at sign for Dry Road Farm, just after auto body garage
5. drive 0.7 mile, park on the right side just past a large barn

Over hill and dale, through rolling farmland, misty swamps, and woodland trails along Blue Marsh Lake—a hike at Dry Road Farm offers a rich variety of sights and sounds. A national historic site owned by the U.S. Army Corps of Engineers, Old Dry Road Farm is operated by several non-profit groups as a living-history farm museum. There are two eighteenth- and nineteenth-century farmsteads and outlying buildings, along with 200 acres of farmland. However, the farmstead buildings are not open to the general public, except for the annual Fall Festival. Old Dry Road Farm has an active program with local schools, and presents demonstration lessons on daily life in colonial rural America and folk arts and crafts.

The acreage is leased privately. On a hike in May we watched planting operations—alfalfa, corn, and soybeans—and spring flowers and shrubs were in bloom along fencerows. Farther along, the wetlands and inlets of the lake provide rich habitat for shorebirds; warblers and songbirds prefer the open meadows.

From the parking lot walk past a metal gate on Highland Road, which is closed to traffic. Game lands are to your left, farm fields to your right; at 0.6 mile you reach an intersection with an abandoned road, Landis Road. Continue straight ahead on the worn gravel road to an intersection with Sterner's Hill Road at 0.7 mile. Continue straight ahead. The road is now dirt and dwindles to a trail along a stand of scrub pines.

Continue straight ahead past a farm road coming in from the right. At 1.2 miles you will reach a sign indicating "Catalpa Trees" and another trail intersection. Catalpa trees, normally a southern variety, don't usually thrive here. These are a species of hardy, or northern, catalpa. They are notable for their large, heart-shaped leaves, white flowers in late spring, and long bean-like seed pods in the fall. Continue straight ahead (north) at the sign.

At 1.6 miles you reach Spring Creek inlet in second-growth woodlands and begin to turn south along Blue Marsh Lake. The trail is marked with blue arrows and hiker symbol signs atop poles. At 2.1 miles a farm road comes in from the right. Continue along a meadow with a wonderful view of the lake. Honeysuckle, multiflora rose, sumac, and even wild lilac bloom here in May. This area is alive with finches and warblers, including yellow warblers, cardinals, and song sparrows—who are heard as well as seen.

After crossing a wooden bridge over a small stream, the trail follows switchbacks to climb 100 feet up a hill. As the trail levels off you reach Sterner's Hill Road again at 3.3 miles. A right turn here leads back to Highland Road, shortening the hike to 5.2 miles.

Walk along cultivated fields, then cross two wooden footbridges. A slow-moving stream winds through marshland on the left. The yellow loose-strife, skunk cabbage, and Jack-in-the-pulpit here bloom in May, and dogwood grows along the wood's edge. At a sign for Dry Road Farm at 5.4 miles turn left and cross a third bridge. The trail ascends through mixed hardwoods. At the top of a rise look for a farm road through the trees on the right. Turn off the trail onto a 30-foot-long path and then right again onto the farm road.

At 5.9 miles you reach Highland Road. Turn right. Raspberries and blackberries along the road provide a tasty snack in July and August. But watch out for the poison ivy! An opportunistic plant, poison ivy and its relatives thrive in highly disturbed locations such as along fencerows, at field edges, and in moist areas along most of this hike. Return to the parking lot and your car at 6.3 miles.

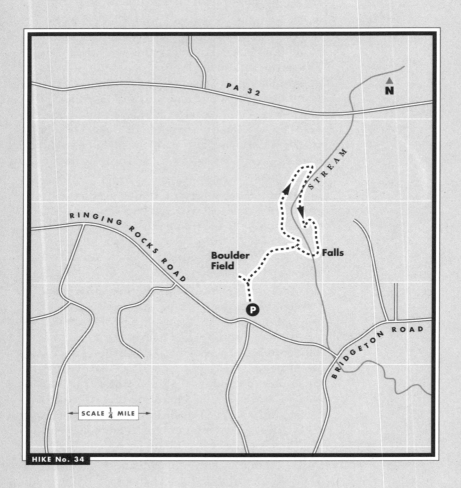

PA 32

N

STREAM

RINGING ROCKS ROAD

Boulder
Field

Falls

P

BRIDGETON ROAD

SCALE ¼ MILE

HIKE No. 34

Ringing Rocks

No. 34

For information only   **Bucks County Department of Parks and Recreation**

Core Creek Park, 901 East Bridgetown Pike,
Langhorne, PA 19047; (215) 757-0571 or 348-6114

Distance	1.5 miles
Elevation	270 feet
Time to hike	1½ hours
Surface	rocky trail
Interesting features	70-acre wooded park with wildflowers; largest "ringing" boulder field in Pennsylvania; waterfall in a hemlock grove
Facilities	rest rooms, picnic tables at parking lot; no water
Disability access	no
Hunting	no

Directions   **from US 202 near New Britain, Pa:**

1. drive north on PA 611 for 16.9 miles to Center Hill Road
2. turn right onto Center Hill Road, drive 3.1 miles to Ringing Rocks Road
3. turn right onto Ringing Rocks Road, drive 0.9 mile to the park entrance on the left

Ringing Rocks is a boulder field, a leftover from the last glacial period of 20,000 years ago. Several other boulder fields exist in Pennsylvania—one is the River of Rocks near Hawk Mountain Sanctuary, and another is located in Hickory Run State Park in the Poconos. Ringing Rocks is well worth the trip. Besides being the closest boulder field to Philadelphia, Ringing Rocks is unusual in that the boulders here have a distinctive ring when struck by a hammer, owing to their high iron content.

Begin walking at the end of the parking lot. At 200 feet you come to a "Y" intersection; bear right. The trail is fairly level, through a mixed hardwood forest; soon it becomes strewn with ever-larger rocks, then boulders. At 0.1 mile the boulder field comes into view on the left. It is roughly square, 800 feet on a side. You can walk carefully out on the boulders, many of which are red-tinged from their iron content. The rocks farther out are more reddish and seem to ring most clearly when tapped lightly with a hammer. The rocks resonate with varied tones, depending on their iron content, size, and how tightly they are wedged in place. It is actually possible to play a tune on the rocks, an activity children seem especially to enjoy.

Continue to walk slightly downhill on the trail, until at 0.2 mile you reach the edge of a ravine, with car-sized boulders. A tiny stream trickles along at the edge of a 60-foot-wide rock shelf and drops down 30 feet to a ledge below. Turn left along the trail and descend the ravine below the waterfall at 0.4 mile. You are walking on a very flat, smooth, 30- to 50-foot-wide layered rock surface. Continue exploring downstream. The stream bed drops off in a series of 2- to 3-foot-high rock ledges. Then retrace your steps to follow the stream up to the falls. The stream is mostly to your right on the edge of the table-like surface, but some areas of the path along the stream bed are moist and slippery with moss. At the base of the 30-foot falls, look for a trail on your left to climb out of the ravine at 1.1 miles.

Continue exploring upstream for another 0.1 mile or more, stepping over 6-inch-wide cracks in the smooth rock layers. Find the trail again at the top of the waterfall at 1.2 miles and continue back to the edge of the boulder field at 1.4 miles. Return to the "Y" intersection near the start. From here you may take the left fork, which leads to the opposite side of the boulder field. Return to your car at 1.5 miles.

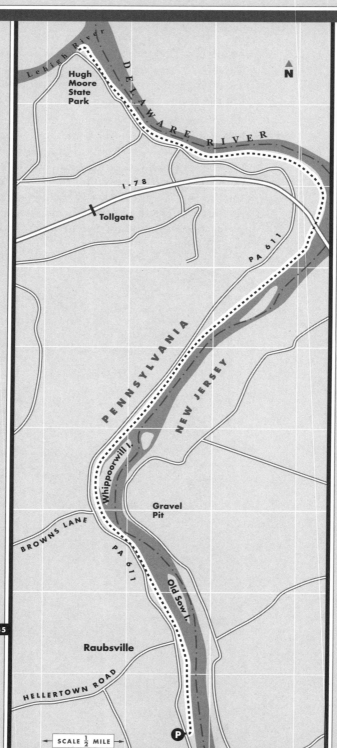

N

Lehigh River

DELAWARE RIVER

Hugh Moore State Park

I-78

Tollgate

PA 611

PENNSYLVANIA

NEW JERSEY

Whippoorwill I.

Gravel Pit

BROWNS LANE

PA 611

Old Sow I.

Raubsville

HELLERTOWN ROAD

P

SCALE ½ MILE

Delaware Canal Towpath

No. 35

For information only	**Delaware Canal State Park** Box 615 A, R.R. 1, Upper Black Eddy, PA 18972 (610) 982-5560
Distance	12.6 miles round trip from Theodore Roosevelt Park at the Ground Hog Lock (locks 22 and 23) to Hugh Moore State Park (lock 24) and return
Elevation	62 feet
Time to hike	4½ hours
Surface	packed earth and grassy towpath
Interesting features	historic Delaware Canal and locks; views across the Delaware River; cross-country skiing
Facilities	water, rest rooms, picnic tables, and grills at Hugh Moore Park; tables and grills only at Theodore Roosevelt Park
Disability access	yes, except for several bridges in Raubsville
Hunting	no

Directions	**from US 202 near New Britain:**
1.	drive north on PA 611 for 25.2 miles
2.	turn right into Theodore Roosevelt Park

Coordinates	40°37'40"N; 75°11'29"W

The Delaware Canal is the only remaining remnant of the great canal system, which along with the Lehigh Canal, led to the development of the coal industry and the rapid industrialization of eastern Pennsylvania in the nineteenth century. The Lehigh Canal brought coal from Mauch Chunk (now Jim Thorpe, Pennsylvania) to Easton; the Delaware Canal, running 60 miles in Bucks County, connected the Lehigh Canal at Easton to tidewater at Bristol. The canal system was built by the state and opened in 1831–1832. After 1866 it was owned and operated by the Lehigh Coal and Navigation Company. With the coming of the railroad, business declined and the canal was closed in 1931. Ownership was transferred back to the state. In 1940 the canal was set aside as the Theodore Roosevelt State Park. Designated a National Historic Landmark in 1978, the canal was renamed the Delaware Canal State Park in 1989.

The southern part of the park is heavily industrialized. This hike at the northern end, from Raubsville to Easton, is more rural. Beginning at Raubsville, at the last lift locks in the 60-mile canal, you walk along the canal towpath north to the locks at Hugh Moore State Park and then return. If you use two cars, you can hike one way for 6.3 miles, or you may simply choose to retrace your steps for a 12.6-mile hike. Either way, your hike will follow a level, easy walking towpath.

Park at the Theodore Roosevelt Recreation and Conservation area. The remains of locks 22 and 23 (Ground Hog Locks) are straight ahead. At the lock the canal narrows into what looks like a metal and wooden chute with wooden gates at each end. A barge entered the chute, the gate behind it was closed, and the water was pumped out of the lock until the barge reached the level of the water downstream. The gate ahead opened, and the barge continued down the canal. Cargo and empty barges were also brought upstream on the canals. The barge moving upstream entered a lock and water was pumped in to raise the barge to the level of the canal ahead. Once in the canal, the barges were towed by mules.

Just to your right the canal empties into a raceway along the river beside the remains of a mill. Cross a wooden footbridge over the canal and turn left on the towpath, with the Delaware River on the right and the canal on the left. At places the canal is filled with water, especially where it is fed by springs from the mountain on your left. At other places it is muddy, even dry and grassy. The canal is almost 50 feet wide from the towpath to the berm on the other side.

At 0.3 mile cross a bridge over the canal, at a 54-mile marker. Several Raubsville homes lie quite close to the towpath, with the river several hundred feet away to the right. At 0.8 mile you walk up a few steps to cross a narrow road.

On the outskirts of Raubsville at 1.3 miles you will pass three small private dwellings on the right. Here the distance between the towpath and the river narrows and the surroundings become more rural. The towpath itself is about 20 feet wide, with a strip of medium-sized hardwoods (oak, maple, yellow-poplars or tuliptrees) and shrubs between the path and the river. Small mammals, including woodchucks and rabbits, as well as ducks and Canada geese are plentiful. You are likely to spot a heron or egret fishing in the canal. A red-bellied turtle may be sunning on logs or rocks. This, the second-largest (average length of 10 to 12 inches) turtle in the Philadelphia area, is considered a threatened species. The largest known population of these turtles in the area is in the Delaware Canal.

Just past milepost 55 at Maxwell walk over a wooden bridge that crosses a concrete spillway. At 2.3 miles you pass the remains of a flow regulator. No longer operational, its wooden gate and conduit controlled water flow between the river and canal. At 3.4 miles Wy-Hit-Tuk Park, a Northampton County Park, is on your left; it is wheelchair accessible by way of a wooden bridge over the canal.

At 4.1 miles pass a bridge and the remains of a gate mechanism over the canal. At 4.2 miles there is another concrete spillway between the river and the canal. At 4.3 miles you walk under the twin bridges of I-78 far above, as it crosses the Delaware from Pennsylvania into New Jersey.

Another wooden bridge crosses the canal at 5.3 miles. Here you also will see another gate mechanism used to control the depth of the water in the canal with pulley and chains. At 6.3 miles you reach lock 24 at Hugh Moore State Park. Across the river is the stone-arch entrance to the Morris Canal on the New Jersey side.

The confluence of the Delaware and Lehigh rivers and the Easton Dam lie straight ahead. To your right is the Easton Dam Fish Passageway Project, a series of fish ladders. Walk down concrete steps to below the water line and observe the fish through windows as they make their way up a series of tanks from the Delaware to the Lehigh River, bypassing the dam. The fish ladder was built in 1993 and has led to the return of shad to the Lehigh River.

Picnic tables and the Canal Museum are straight ahead. The museum is open Monday to Saturday 10:00 a.m. to 4 p.m.; Sunday 1:00 to 5:00 p.m. It is closed New Year's Day, Thanksgiving Day, and Christmas Day. There is a museum admission charge of $1.50 for adults and $0.75 for children. The museum contains exhibits that explain the importance of the Delaware and Lehigh canals to the history of industrial development in the area, as well as a bookstore.

Pick up your second car if you have spotted one here, or retrace your steps back to Theodore Roosevelt Park.

Jacobsburg Settlement

No. 36

Jacobsburg Environmental Education Center

835 Jacobsburg Road, Wind Gap, PA 18091
(610) 746-2801

Distance	4.0 miles
Elevation	260 feet
Time to hike	2 hours
Surface	asphalt path (Henry's Woods Trail); gravel and grassy woods roads, woods trail
Interesting features	Jacobsburg National Historic District—remains of the colonial village of Jacobsburg, John Joseph Henry House and Henry Homestead—restored colonial homes; views from ridge over Bushkill Creek; successional stages of forest regeneration
Facilities	water, rest rooms, picnic facilities at start of hike; picnic tables and rest rooms at site of Jacobsburg
Disability access	the paved Henry's Woods Trail, accessible; the Jacobsburg Trail level to rolling on grassy roads—accessible; the Henry's Woods Trail overlooking Bushkill Creek, not accessible
Hunting	yes

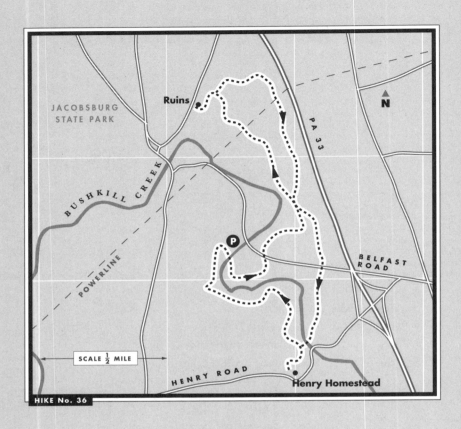

JACOBSBURG
STATE PARK

Ruins

BUSHKILL CREEK

POWERLINE

PA 33

N

P

BELFAST
ROAD

SCALE ½ MILE

HENRY ROAD

Henry Homestead

from northeast extension of Pennsylvania Turnpike (I-476) near Allentown:

1. take exit 33 (toward Allentown), drive east on US 22 for 16.2 miles
2. turn left (north) onto PA 33, 7.0 miles (to Stroudsburg)
3. turn right (east) onto Henry Road (SR 1008) at Belfast, following signs to Jacobsburg State Park; drive 0.1 mile to Belfast Road (SR 1012)
4. turn left onto Belfast Road, drive 0.7 mile
5. park in parking lot on the left

Coordinates   40°46'56"N; 75°17'34"W

The Jacobsburg Environmental Education Center is named for Jacobsburg Settlement, an eighteenth-century community that included a tannery, gristmill, iron forge, and sawmill. It was also the site of a nineteenth-century gun industry. This fairly challenging hike also offers a steep climb and a view over Bushkill Creek from a high ridge, as well as the historic buildings and ruins of Jacobsburg.

Leave the parking lot, walking south on a wooden footbridge (accessible) across Bushkill Creek. Just on the other side of the bridge there are rest rooms to the left and a sign indicating the asphalt Henry's Woods Nature Trail to the right. At 0.2 mile you leave the mixed hardwoods to enter a mature hemlock forest next to the creek. The trail is fairly easy walking. The trail is at first asphalt, then packed earth, then gravel; it is marked with orange squares on short wooden posts.

At 0.3 mile you reach a trail intersection. The Henry's Woods Trail continues straight ahead; turn left onto the red-blazed Jacobsburg Trail, which continues to the site of the ruins of

Jacobsburg village. It is crossed several times by an equestrian trail marked with yellow arrows. At each crossing, bear left to follow the Jacobsburg Trail.

You will find wildflowers along the grassy path that passes through a field overgrown with shrubs and small trees. At 0.4 mile you cross Belfast Road, then a gravel access road. At 0.7 mile you will cross a 5-foot-wide stream on a wooden footbridge. Continue to bear left on the trail marked with red squares on wooden posts, through fields in various stages of forest succession.

At 0.9 mile you enter a mature hardwood forest, a mixture of oaks and hickories. At 1.0 mile you pass through a power line cut. At 1.4 miles cross a 15-foot-wide tributary of Bushkill Creek on a wooden footbridge. At 1.5 miles you reach a picnic grove, with tables and rest rooms.

Abandoned towns abound in Pennsylvania, but unlike the ghost towns of the West, they are quickly overgrown with vegetation and evidence can be hard to find. If you look closely around the area, you should be able to spot the stone foundations of the colonial village of Jacobsburg.

Turn back to return, crossing the stream again at 1.6 miles. Turn left just after the stream, to follow the equestrian trail marked with yellow arrows. (This trail becomes narrower and is prone to being muddy. The wheeled hiker may prefer to proceed straight ahead on the Jacobsburg Trail, which is marked with red squares.)

At 1.8 miles pass under the power line again, then reenter the woods. At 2.0 miles you come to another power line cut adjacent to PA 33. Follow the equestrian trail that parallels the road and power line cut. At 2.2 miles you rejoin the Jacobsburg Trail. At 2.5 miles look closely for the foundation remains of more colonial buildings and a springhouse. At 2.6 miles pass on old red barn on the left and cross Belfast Road again.

You reach a T intersection with the asphalt-paved Henry's Woods Trail at 2.8 miles; turn left. Cross a small stream on a wooden footbridge. Turn right on the orange-blazed Homestead Trail. A wide gravel path runs alongside the stream.

At 3.0 miles cross Bushkill Creek on a wooden footbridge (not accessible to wheeled traffic because of perpendicular wooden slats on the steep approach to the bridge). Turn left after crossing the bridge on the Homestead Trail. At 3.1 miles you reach a parking lot and several restored colonial buildings. The 1812 Henry Homestead and the 1832 John Joseph Henry House are open to the public on the fourth Sunday of each month from April through October; the hours are from 1:00 to 5:00 p.m. Nearby is the site of the Boulton Gun Factory. William Henry II manufactured guns here for the War of 1812.

Retrace your steps to the bridge. The combined Homestead and Henry's Woods trails continue uphill. At 3.3 miles you reach the top of a fairly steep climb, where the trail splits. The blue-blazed Homestead Trail continues straight ahead and follows the top of the ridge. It is a safer course for those with young children, unsure footing, or a fear of heights.

The Henry's Woods Trail, marked with a sign warning of hazardous conditions ahead, turns right. It is blazed with orange squares on short posts. The trail follows the ridgeline one-quarter from the top, along a very steep hemlock-covered slope with a precipitous drop 200 feet below to the Bushkill Creek. The trail is fortunately well-maintained and leveled with boards, but there is no fence to prevent a fall.

Cross a tributary over a wooden footbridge and then descend from the ridge on wooden steps at 3.8 miles. Pass a small stage and amphitheater on the left. At 4.0 miles you reach the parking lot and your car.

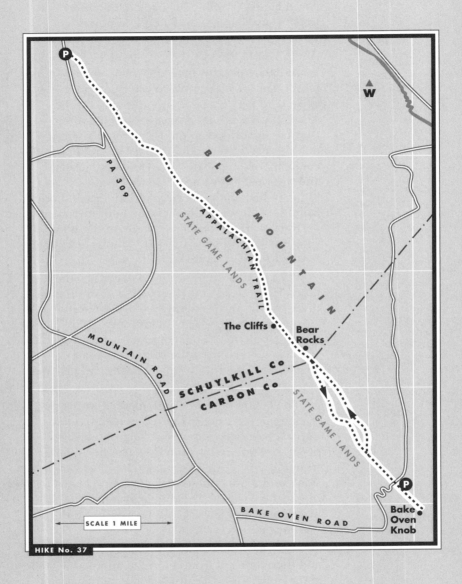

P

W

B L U E   M O U N T A I N

PA 309

APPALACHIAN TRAIL

STATE GAME LANDS

The Cliffs ●   Bear
Rocks ●

MOUNTAIN ROAD

SCHUYLKILL Co.

CARBON Co.

STATE GAME LANDS

P

Bake
Oven
Knob ●

BAKE OVEN ROAD

SCALE 1 MILE

Bake Oven Knob, Bear Rocks, and The Cliffs

No 37

For information only **Pennsylvania State Game Lands Number 217, Lehigh County**

Southeast Region Headquarters (800) 228-0791

Distance	11.2 miles
Elevation	400 feet
Time to hike	5¾ hours
Surface	very rocky woods trail
Interesting features	scenic views; bird watching; rock climbing
Facilities	none
Disability access	no
Hunting	yes

Directions **from northeast extension of Pennsylvania Turnpike (I-476) near Allentown:**

1. take exit 33 to US 22 east, drive 0.8 mile (follow signs to PA 309 north—Tamaqua)
2. take PA 309 north, drive 18.5 miles to the top of Blue Mountain; parking lot for Appalachian Trail is on the right

Coordinates 40°42'25"N; 75°48'26"W

Bake Oven Knob, Bear Rocks, and The Cliffs make for a very challenging hike on the Appalachian Trail. Be sure to wear sturdy hiking boots, as you will be scrambling over many large boulders and sharp rocks. Bake Oven Knob is also an excellent hawk lookout, similar to the well-known Hawk Mountain Sanctuary, which is located 15 miles to the southwest along the Kittatinny Ridge. However, Bake Oven Knob is much less crowded on fall weekends, and, unlike the privately owned Hawk Mountain Sanctuary, there is no admission fee.

From the parking lot follow blue blazes east for 50 feet, then turn left on the white-blazed Appalachian Trail. Almost all of this hike is through mixed hardwood forest, with many varieties of oak, hickory, beech, and mountain laurel. At first you are on a narrow trail, which is joined at 0.5 mile by an old rocky woods road. At 2.0 miles you reach a power line cut on the top of the ridge, with lovely views of the Lehigh River Valley to the north (left) and the Schuylkill River Valley to the south (right).

Here the woods road ends. The trail becomes progressively rockier and your footing is more difficult. If you look up, you notice the mountain ridge has become narrower. At 2.5 miles you reach a large rock outcropping on the right, with long views of Allentown and Bethlehem in the distance. This is a good place to watch for raptors riding air currents rising along the side of the mountain, searching for prey. We watched three turkey vultures, gliding back and forth before us only 20 feet away, with hardly a flapping of their huge wings (they have a 6-foot wingspan).

At 3.0 miles another huge rock outcropping rises to the right, The Cliffs, and you find yourself climbing over the granite boulders for more spectacular views to the south. This is not altogether pleasant for someone with a fear of heights or a balance problem. It is very windy atop the high, narrow ridge, which gives you a sensation of being lifted off your feet. It is possible to do as we did and walk to the left, around the outcropping. However, even here, you must watch your step as you maneuver over and around the boulders.

As you continue the hardwoods give way to large hemlock trees. In deep shade, and with the wind, the temperature drops perceptibly. At 3.5 miles notice another high (300-foot) rocky outcropping on the left—Bear Rocks. The Appalachian Trail doesn't lead over these rocks. However, if you were earlier able to scramble over The Cliffs, you may find that the 240-degree view over farmland from these rocks is worth the short detour.

At 3.6 miles the trail again becomes a rocky woods road. Notice a trail leading to the left, with white blazes on the trees; this is an alternate return route. Continue straight ahead on the Appalachian Trail. At 4.6 miles you come to a T intersection with a woods road; bear right, staying on the white-blazed Appalachian Trail. At 5.0 miles cross Bake Oven Road, a gravel road, with two adjoining parking lots. (This is a parking area used by Bake Oven Knob bird-watchers.)

Continue on the Appalachian Trail. It becomes steeper and rockier as you climb to 1600 feet, reaching Bake Oven Knob at 5.6 miles. From here, you have a panoramic view of 270 degrees to the valleys 1,000 feet below, and you can observe the hawks on their fall migratory routes. September is the best time to see broad-winged hawks, ospreys, and possibly bald eagles. In October you will see the greatest variety of hawks, especially red-tailed. Golden eagles are sometimes spotted in November. You will see fewer hawks in spring, but at that season you are likely to see turkey vultures and migrating warblers.

Turn around and retrace your steps. For a different return route, at 6.6 miles proceed straight ahead at the woods road at the T intersection described earlier. This leads through an area of second-growth woods. Many of the trees have been cut and attempts made to propagate pine seedlings, which are grown in plastic tubes to protect them from the deer. At 7.1 miles look for a trail to the left, with a small sign pointing to Bear Rocks. The trail is not well maintained; follow the white blazes on the trees, which mark the edge of a property line within the State Game Lands. (A section of private property is on the right.)

At 7.6 miles you again reach the Appalachian Trail. Continue on the return route past The Cliffs to return to your car at 11.2 miles.

Directions **To reach Bake Oven Knob via Bake Oven Road, for a round-trip hike of 1.2 miles from the parking lot—from the northeast extension of the Pennsylvania Turnpike (I-476) near Allentown:**

1. take exit 33 to US 22 east, drive 0.8 mile (follow signs to PA 309 north—Tamaqua)
2. take PA 309 north, drive 15.5 miles to Mountain Road (SR 4024)
3. turn right, drive 2.8 miles to Bake Oven Road (SR 4019)
4. turn left, follow the signs for Bake Oven Road; drive 2.2 miles to the parking lot on the top of Blue Mountain

Coordinates 40°44'22"N; 75°44'50"W

The Pinnacle and Pulpit Rock

No. 38

For information only **Pennsylvania State Game Lands Number 106, Lehigh County**

Southeast Region Headquarters (800) 228-0791

Distance	9.0 miles
Elevation	1,000 feet
Time to hike	5 hours
Surface	very rocky trail
Interesting features	a challenging hike on the Appalachian Trail, including a 1,000-foot climb in 2 miles; scenic views from two locations at the top of Blue Mountain
Facilities	no water; portable toilet at astronomical observatory (at 7.0 miles)
Disability access	no
Hunting	yes

Directions **from US 202 near King of Prussia:**

1. take US 422 west (toward Pottsville–Reading), drive 40.0 miles to US 222

2. turn right (north) onto US 222, drive 1.8 miles to PA 61

3. turn left (north) onto PA 61, drive 13.0 miles to sign for Hamburg

(continued)

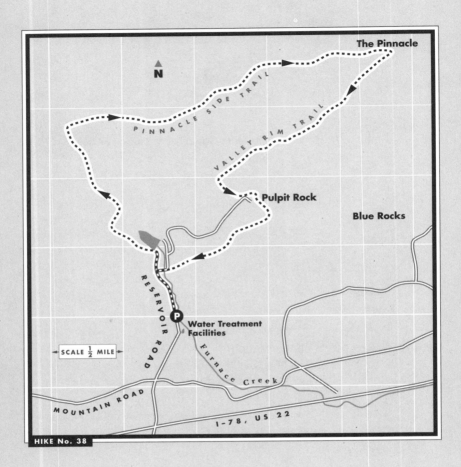

The Pinnacle

N

PINNACLE SIDE TRAIL

VALLEY RIM TRAIL

Pulpit Rock

Blue Rocks

RESERVOIR ROAD

P Water Treatment
Facilities

SCALE ½ MILE

Furnace Creek

MOUNTAIN ROAD

I-78, US 22

HIKE No. 38

4. bear right on South Fourth Street, drive 1.0 mile to State Street (old Route 22)

5. turn right onto State Street, drive 2.3 miles to Reservoir Road (just past St. Paul's Church on the right)

6. turn left onto Reservoir Road, drive 1.0 mile, park in front of fence

Coordinates 40° 34'54"N; 75°56'33"W

The Pinnacle, Blue Mountain, and the Sand Spring–Tom Lowe Trails are farther away from Philadelphia than the other hikes, and it may take you an hour and a half to reach the trailheads for these hikes. However, you will find the drive well worth it if you are seeking a physical challenge and truly spectacular mountain views. Be sure to wear hiking boots with good ankle support, as you will be scrambling over rocky trails.

To reach The Pinnacle, park near an area enclosed by chain-link fencing—water treatment facilities for the Hamburg Reservoir. Following a trail to your left around the fence, you reach a gravel road. Continue up the road for 0.3 mile to Windsor Furnace, the remains of a nineteenth-century iron-smelting furnace. The Appalachian Trail crosses the road at a trail sign. Your return route is on the trail coming in from the right. For now, bear left (south) on the Appalachian Trail for just 300 feet. The Appalachian Trail then turns left; you will continue straight ahead (north) on a blue-blazed trail.

At 0.4 mile you reach the Hamburg Reservoir. Although there is a weathered no-trespassing sign, you may walk around the gate along the reservoir. The blue-blazed trail shortly turns left away from the reservoir. Although the road is fairly steep, it is still fairly easy walking through maple, birch, and oak woods. As you climb you will notice that the leafy canopy thins, allowing more light to reach the ground. Ferns, huckleberry, and stunted mountain laurel cover the forest floor.

Where the trail begins leveling off at the top of the mountain, you reach the Appalachian Trail again at 2.0 miles. Turn right (east) on the white-blazed Appalachian Trail, on a woods road. At 2.6 miles note the sign for Gold Spring, a seasonal spring down a path 100 feet to the right. The road ends at 4.0 miles and continues as a narrow trail, which becomes progressively rockier. At 4.6 miles, amid a jumble of huge boulders, bear left following blue blazes for 250 feet to The Pinnacle. Watch your step as you walk over to the edge of the precipice for 180-degree views of farmland below. On a recent visit we counted ten hawks at eye level and below riding the wind currents in search of prey. To the south, notice an expanse of rocks, Blue Rocks. Like Ringing Rocks (see Hike 34), this band of rocks 500 feet wide and a half-mile long was formed during the last ice age. Huge glaciers scoured the earth and deposited these boulders. Composed of hard quartzite, they have resisted erosion. Summer vegetation obscures the size of the boulder field somewhat from this location. You will also see Blue Rocks, but at a different angle, from Pulpit Rock.

Return to the Appalachian Trail and continue on what was once called the Valley Rim Trail, along the edge of the mountain. You will pass several rock fields and outcroppings on the left, with limited views to the valley. Sharp-edged rocks of many sizes, protruding from the ground and impossible to avoid, can be felt even through hiking boots and threaten to twist an ankle. The trail follows the rim of the mountain to reach Pulpit Rock at 7.0 miles. Here you have an even better view of Blue Rocks.

On the other side of the trail note the astronomical observatory through the trees. (A shortcut here on the observatory road leads back to the parking lot at 8.0 miles.)

As you continue on the rocky trail, watch for the white blazes painted on the rocks. They lead left, across a pile of boulders to descend steeply over natural stone steps and switchbacks. At 7.5 miles the footing becomes easier on an old woods road. At 8.4 miles turn left onto a wider woods road at an intersection with a trail leading to the Windsor Furnace overnight shelter to the right.

The walking from here is fairly smooth and level; you will cross a small stream and the gravel road to the observatory. Complete the loop at Windsor Furnace at 8.7 miles and turn left to return to your car at 9.0 miles. Although quite popular with hiking clubs and scout groups, The Pinnacle and Pulpit Rock remain natural and unspoiled hiking destinations.

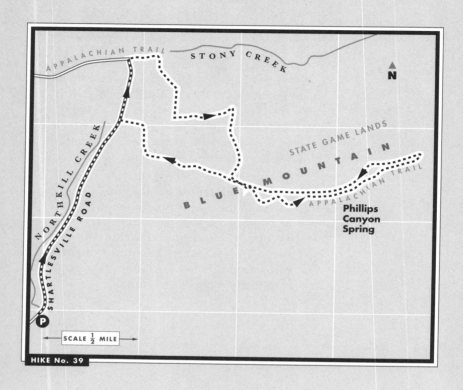

APPALACHIAN TRAIL

STONY CREEK

N

NORTHKILL CREEK

STATE GAME LANDS

BLUE MOUNTAIN

APPALACHIAN TRAIL

SHARTLESVILLE ROAD

Phillips
Canyon
Spring

P

SCALE ½ MILE

HIKE No. 39

Blue Mountain and Phillips Canyon

No. 39

For information only Pennsylvania State Game Lands Number 110, Berks County

Southeast Region Headquarters (800) 228-0791

Distance	8.3 miles
Elevation	1200 feet
Time to hike	4½ hours
Surface	rocky woods trail; dirt road
Interesting features	a very challenging hike on the Appalachian Trail; steep climbs; diverse animal and bird populations
Facilities	none
Disability access	no
Hunting	yes

Directions **from US 202 near King of Prussia:**

1. drive west on US 422 (toward Pottsville–Reading) for 40.0 miles to US 222

2. turn right (north) onto US 222, drive 1.8 miles to PA 61

3. turn left (north) onto PA 61, drive 14.5 miles to I-78

4. turn left (west) onto I-78, drive 6.5 miles to exit 8 (Shartlesville)

(continued)

5. turn right (north) onto Mountain Road (SR 411), drive 0.3 mile

6. continue straight ahead on Forge Dam Road for 1.1 miles, bear right on Shartlesville Road to enter the state game land area

7. continue another 0.5 mile, park at parking lot at a gate

Coordinates 40°32'15"N; 76°07'25"W

This rugged hike, within State Game Lands Number 110, is a good example of how good forest management improves both the diversity and success of wildlife. Deer graze in open grassy meadows running along the top of Blue Mountain. Low shrubs along the woods edge and brush cuttings provide cover and food for songbirds as well as game birds. Feedlots and feeding stations support the wildlife during rough winters. You are likely to see many types of animals and birds on this remote mountain hike.

Take plenty of water, wear sturdy hiking boots, and be prepared for a drop in temperature of 10 to 15 degrees atop Blue Mountain. From the parking lot walk uphill, with Northkill Creek on your left, through a hemlock and rhododendron forest. The game lands road is well marked with orange diamonds tacked to trees. At 0.1 mile pass the sign for the Sand Spring Trail on your left (see Hike 40). Continue straight ahead. As you climb, the soil becomes sandy and dry, and the thick vegetation thins out to second-growth hardwoods.

As you top a rise at 1.0 mile, notice a service road coming in from the right; this will be your return route. Feedlots for turkey and deer on both sides of the road are stocked in the winter by the game commission. Continue straight ahead, past another trail intersection and a sign for the Wieser State Forest. Walk around the metal gate and

Blue Mountain and Phillips Canyon

continue straight ahead, reaching the Appalachian Trail at 1.3 miles.

From here you have glimpses of the valleys to the north and south through the trees. Turn right (east) on the Appalachian Trail, winding through a mature oak forest. You will step across several intermittent streams. Blueberries, ripe in mid-summer, grow in thick bushes along the trail. The trail gradually becomes rockier and downright rugged. At 2.1 miles follow a turn sharply right and straight up, climbing 200 feet in 0.3 mile over outcroppings of quartzite. The trail levels off as you reach the top of the ridgeline, and you will find yourself stepping out suddenly into an open meadow along the crest of the mountain.

This is a good place to stop for a rest. Paper birch, Eastern redcedars, and scrub oak flourish along the meadow edge. Raspberries and blackberries are abundant in late summer. You may see deer along the edge of the woods emerging to browse.

Cross the service road at 2.5 miles and reenter the woods. The trail is quite rocky; it is necessary to step carefully around and over some outcroppings of sharp quartzite and smoother sandstone. Watching our feet, we were startled to nearly step on a 5-foot-long black rat snake lying directly over the trail. He was rather sluggish, for it was a cool, early April morning. With thick vegetation and boulders on both sides of the trail, we had to literally lift him out of the way with a stick so we could proceed. Rat snakes are not poisonous; they kill their prey by constriction. They occupy the same habitat as diamondback rattlesnakes.

At 4.0 miles you reach a sign for the Phillips Canyon spring, 135 yards to your right. Following the unmarked path, you find the ground suddenly drops away to a steep declivity in the side of the mountain. Runoff from the mountain has carved a deep, narrow V-shaped gorge lined with huge boulders. If you bear to the left of the V, descending 100 feet from the top, you will find a seasonal spring arising from deep inside the mountain. The trail is so steep you must use your hands and feet to scramble over the rocks. Watch for snakes!

Returning to the Appalachian Trail to continue; you will encounter a blue-blazed trail crossing the trail at 5.0 miles. (A left turn here will lead back to the service road and shorten the hike to a total of 7.5 miles.) Continuing straight ahead on the Appalachian Trail through mixed oaks, poplar, and cedar, you reach the open area at the top of the ridge again at 6.3 miles. Turn left on the service road, leaving the Appalachian Trail. A 30- to 50-foot-wide mown swath alongside the road affords long views of the mountains to the east and west. At 7.0 miles you reach the Appalachian Trail crossing. At the top of the last rise you have lovely views to the mountains to the north and west. From here the trail slopes downhill alongside brush and dense shrubs. These are favorite nesting places for quail, pheasant, and ruffed grouse, Pennsylvania's state bird. Thrushes and warblers also find cover as well as food.

At 7.3 miles you reach the game lands road; turn left to return to your car at 8.3 miles.

Sand Spring–Tom Lowe Trail

For information only **Pennsylvania State Game Lands Number110, Berks County**

Southeast Region Headquarters (800) 228-0791

Distance	4.5 miles
Elevation	850 feet
Time to hike	3 hours
Surface	very rocky in places; sometimes steep
Interesting features	tumbling streams; springs; deep hemlock ravines and slopes
Facilities	water at Sand Spring at 1.7 miles; no other facilities
Disability access	no
Hunting	yes

Directions **from US 202 near King of Prussia:**

1. drive west on US 422 (toward Pottsville–Reading) for 40.0 miles to US 222

2. turn right (north) onto US 222, drive 1.8 miles to PA 61

3. turn left (north) onto PA 61, drive 14.5 miles to I-78

4. turn left (west) onto I-78, drive 6.5 miles to exit 8 (Shartlesville)

(continued)

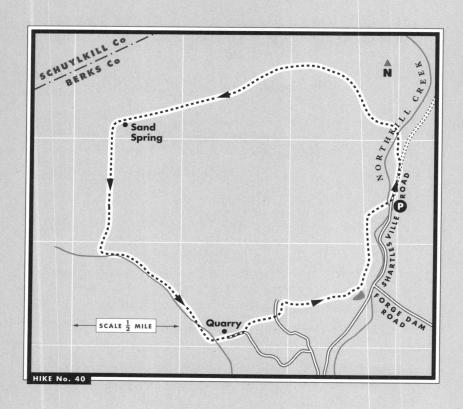

SCHUYLKILL Co.
BERKS Co.

Sand
Spring

N

NORTHKILL CREEK

P

SHARTLESVILLE ROAD

SCALE ½ MILE

Quarry

FORGE DAM ROAD

HIKE No. 40

190

5. turn right (north) onto Mountain Road (SR 411), drive 0.3 mile

6. continue straight ahead on Forge Dam Road for 1.1 miles, bear right on Shartlesville Road to enter the state game land area

7. continue another 0.5 mile, park at parking lot at a gate

Coordinates 40°32'15"N; 76°07'25"W

This second wilderness hike in State Game Lands Number 110 offers tumbling streams and thick hemlock and rhododendron forest. You are likely to spot deer, porcupine, turtles, and other wildlife. Just before reaching the parking lot, note the orange blazes for the Tom Lowe Trail on the left along the stream—this will be your return route.

Begin walking north, past the gate, up a gravel road. Northkill Creek runs along the road on the left side. Hemlock, mixed hardwoods, and thick rhododendron predominate. At 0.1 mile turn left on the blue-blazed Sand Spring Trail, which is marked with a sign.

At 0.3 mile cross Northkill Creek. From here, you climb steeply out of the ravine to an area of mixed hardwoods. The trail levels out at 100 to 200 feet below the top of the ridgeline on your right. At 0.9 mile the trail again descends through hemlocks and rhododendrons. You step over many small streams and springs, then ascend once again through mixed hardwoods. As you climb, the small hardwoods thin out; the ground here is covered with huckleberry plants. At 1.7 miles reach the walled Sand Spring, containing fresh water at most times of the year.

The Sand Spring Trail bears right and continues 0.7 mile to the top of the ridge and the

Appalachian Trail. However, straight ahead on the other side of the spring, look for the orange-blazed Tom Lowe Trail. From here, your trail continues straight ahead through mixed hardwood forest. At 1.8 miles the trail begins to descend, dropping 300 feet in 0.4 mile, on a very rocky slope. The hemlocks here are smaller, with more hardwoods and laurel.

At 2.5 miles you will cross a lovely stream on stepping stones. The slopes are covered with large hemlocks, with openings permitting views to your left on several streams below, with many small waterfalls. The trail continues along the stream, turning left to enter Little Valley at 3.0 miles.

After walking through an area of many ferns and fewer trees, you cross several seasonal streams and springs. You will encounter many blowdowns, which make it all too easy to step off the trail. Watch carefully for the double blazes indicating turns.

At 3.2 miles you will enter a clearing with an old gravel quarry on your left. Follow the gravel service road another 0.1 mile and watch for the orange blaze on your left, signaling a turn uphill to enter the woods again. The trail is quite rocky and sometimes steep uphill. At 3.5 miles the trail crosses a rocky area with many small springs. You can hear the sounds of an underground stream.

There is a sharp left turn at 3.8 miles, and another sharp left turn at 3.9 miles. You can see a pond in the clearing on your right at 4.0 miles. At 4.1 miles the trail descends through a thick grove of hemlocks; here the trail is basically a stream bed in places. You come to the edge of the Northkill Creek on your right at 4.2 miles. The trail turns left, climbing up a ridge, then down a short rocky slope.

Cross Northkill Creek at 4.3 miles, stepping over on rocks near the ruins of a bridge. Continue following the orange blazes with the stream on your left until you reach the parking lot at 4.5 miles.

HIKES ▶ Around Philadelphia ▶ Appendices

Hikes by Length

5.0 to 10.0 miles

Over 10 miles

Hikes by Disability Access

Partially accessible

No. 2 Scott Arboretum
7 Schuylkill Center for Environmental Education
9 Wissahickon Gorge
12 Neshaminy Park
13 Delhaas Woods and Silver Lake
14 Churchville Nature Center
19 Betzville Railroad Grade–Schuylkill River Trail
20 Valley Forge
26 Nolde Forest
29 Peace Valley
30 Bowman's Hill State Wildflower Preserve
35 Delaware Canal Towpath
36 Jacobsburg Settlement

Completely accessible from start to finish

No. 1 Heinz Wildlife Refuge
4 Leiper–Smedley Trail
6 Ridley Creek
16 Tyler State Park
21 Struble Trail

Hike Map Index

The U.S. Geological Survey maps (7.5 minute quadrangles) from which the maps of the forty hikes are derived are listed here, by hike number and name.

No. 1   Heinz Wildlife Refuge..............................*Lansdowne*

2   Scott Arboretum.......................................*Lansdowne*

3   Springfield Trail ....*Lansdowne*

4   Leiper–Smedley Trail..............................*Lansdowne*

5   Tyler Arboretum ....*Media*

6   Ridley Creek..*Media*

7   Schuylkill Center for Environmental Education...........................*Norristown/Germantown*

8   Andorra Natural Area ....*Germantown*

9   Wissahickon Gorge ....*Germantown*

10   Lorimer Park ....*Frankford*

11   Pennypack Wilderness ....*Hatboro*

12   Neshaminy Park ....*Beverly NJ–Pa*

13   Delhaas Woods and Silver Lake ....*Bristol Pa–NJ*

14   Churchville Nature Center........................*Langhorne*

15   Five-Mile Woods Preserve ....*Trenton West NJ–Pa*

16   Tyler State Park..*Langhorne*

17   Audubon Wildlife Sanctuary.................................*Collegeville/Valley Forge*

Hikes Near Public Transportation

Please call SEPTA (215) 580-7800 for current routes and schedule information.